CHANGE FATIGUE

CHANGE FATIGUE

CHANGE FATIGUE

FLIP TEAMS FROM BURNOUT TO BUY-IN

JENNY MAGIC
MELISSA BREKER

ISBN 979-8-9882097-2-0 Hardcover
ISBN 979-8-9882097-0-6 Paperback
ISBN 979-8-9882097-1-3 eBook
Library of Congress Control Number:
9798988209706

Dark Lightning Press
8868 Research Blvd #301
Austin, TX 78757

Edited by Maggie Frank-Hsu
Cover and interior design by Joanna Holden

changefatigue.com

FOR EVERY LEADER
WHO KNOWS
THERE HAS TO
BE A BETTER WAY
TO CHANGE.

CONTENTS

CONTENTS

PREFACE

EVERYONE IS EXHAUSTED.

PICTURE THIS...

Bianca's role as a marketing assistant includes keeping the executive team updated on the status of high-priority projects. Every quarter, she sends an Excel spreadsheet to dozens of project owners asking for updates, which she then dutifully transcribes into an extensive PDF document for the meeting.

Her boss, Gina, suggests switching from this tedious process to a shared online tool where project owners would keep their items updated at their convenience, eliminating hours of work and urgent artificial deadlines. Even though it would save her tons of time, Bianca resists, knowing that requiring project owners to use a new tool will not go over well. She feels it's easier just to do it herself, even if the process takes much longer. Her boss is at a loss: why wouldn't Bianca want a change that would result in less work?

Every time leaders introduce a new technology, process, or way of working, they are asking their teams to change.

BUT EXHAUSTED TEAMS RESIST CHANGE.

How did things get this bad? *Change Fatigue* is a term most business leaders have heard, either because they're actively dealing with it, or because they're trying to figure out how to avoid making it worse. When we talk about change fatigue in this book, here is what we mean.

For one, most employees have had experiences with change in the workplace that have left them feeling undervalued and stretched thin. Often change moves forward in their workplaces only because executives push managers, who push their employees, without asking for input or providing any explanation. Add to that the impact of a global pandemic that forced rushed and ill-considered changes into place just to keep work, school, and life limping along, and even high performers and formerly "early adopters" are wary of jumping on the bandwagon for any new change initiatives.

Change fatigue always comes as lots of small changes happen independently, piling up on staff who are facing change on multiple fronts. The volume of small requests to use a new tool, try a new process, or change how work gets done might seem minor but it really adds up, and can greatly impact individual willingness to change.

All of this to say: everyone is exhausted. Change fatigue is real, and it makes sense, but change still has to happen. There's no way around it: evolution— *change*—is a necessary function of every living thing, and organizations are no exception. If a team is not evolving, innovating, and showing value they will likely find themselves on the budgetary chopping block. The status quo is not a viable solution.

So, change has to happen. But we don't have to accept that change has to be so exhausting.

Leaders need to account for how a change initiative actually impacts the people making the change. This means planning the right activities in the right order with the right people involved, well before announcing anything to the whole team. This kind of preparation allows teams to adopt and sustain change more reliably.

In other words, if you don't un-frustrate your team, you're not going to get where you want to go.

That's why we wrote this book: to provide you, the change leader, with the preparation and tools to roll out change without sacrificing your team's morale or sanity. Successful transformation includes a plan not just for the change (*what we're doing*) and the implementation (*how we're doing it*), but also the sustainable, long-term adoption of the change (*who is going to keep doing it*).

— What exactly needs to be done differently?
— How is it going to get done?
— Who is going to do it (and keep it going)?

Another often overlooked aspect is the important question of measurement. (*How will we know if it worked?*) Identifying new critical behaviors leaders will use to assess success will help everyone know whether they are on track to deliver the change successfully.

THIS BOOK IS HERE TO HELP YOUR TEAM FIND A BETTER WAY TO WORK.

— **Craft** a roadmap for sustainable change (a clear North Star to transformation).
— **Generate** engagement and buy-in from your teams.
— **Navigate** and name the impacts of the change.
— **Build** happier, more innovative teams along the way.

WHO THIS BOOK IS FOR

If your organization needs to do something differently and you're stalled, stuck, or frustrated with the process, this book is for you.

Examples of the kind of change or new initiative you might be considering:

— Updating the strategic vision of your organization
— Reorganizing staff or departments to meet new goals
— Aligning sales and marketing teams
— Implementing or switching project management tools or other technology
— Redesigning your organization's website
— Changing how teams run meetings, communicate during the workday, or share files

... or anything else that requires teams to get out of their routines and do things differently.

CAVEAT: if you have a major, complex change over a long period of time that impacts hundreds or thousands of people, this book is probably just the starting point as you prepare for an intricate change. There is an entire discipline of Change Management dedicated to this scale of change. (Find more Change Management resources at changefatigue.com.)

That said, smaller changes on the scale of three to six months that change the day-to-day jobs of up to a few dozen people deserve change support too.

These small to midsize changes can add up to major innovations for your organization, but they're often neglected in change planning. This is a handbook to guide you, the change leader, through the necessary thinking to give your change the best chance of success.

We (Jenny and Melissa) have each spent the last 20 years advising companies—from a dozen employees to Fortune 100—on marketing and digital transformations, and the last five years specializing in heading off the mistakes most organizations make when leading those transformations. In addition to our consulting practices, we're also both professional coaches and experienced facilitators with supporting certifications in change management and benchmarking team performance.

These ideas and approaches have been tested on lots of teams of all sizes and skill levels at a wide variety of organizations. There's no silver bullet for making change effortless, but there are plenty of best practices to make change easier.

A NOTE ON KEY TERMS

Change fatigue is a feeling of apathy or resistance to a proposed change in the workplace. Change fatigue is a significant barrier to innovation, and unfortunately it is all too common. By actively addressing it, leaders can remove the real barriers to change and increase engagement. As you move forward, consider these three areas of change support you might need.

Change management is the umbrella term for all approaches to prepare, support, and help individuals, teams, and organizations in making organizational change. Change managers can also be referred to as change leaders. Change leaders may be internal staff or outside consultants, responsible for determining the scope and timelines for a change initiative that a project manager then oversees. The investment in dedicated change management resources will vary depending on the scale of the change initiative.

Project management focuses on the day-to-day accountability for any project. Project managers typically don't write change plans; they break down large tasks into smaller ones, assign and manage workload, and follow up with stakeholders to ensure tasks are completed. (In this book we refer to any staff in your organization who will be impacted by the change or whose support is essential as stakeholders. These people are key to the success of your project.)

Change facilitation often happens early, as part of the discovery phase of work, to assess the cultural, organizational, and team requirements for the change. Change facilitation is a subset of change management that focuses on communicating change and engaging team members to ensure they are ready to change and have the support they need to do so. They also help craft the change narrative so that it is as persuasive to stakeholders as possible. Change facilitators work closely with change leaders and project managers to refine the scope and timelines based on feedback from stakeholders and best practices. On smaller projects without a dedicated change management team, change facilitators bridge the gap between change leaders and stakeholders.

THIS BOOK IS FOCUSED ON CHANGE FACILITATION.

INTRODUCTION

Are They *Willing* to Change?

A December 2022 report by global consulting firm AlixPartners found that 75 percent of CEOs are anxious that their company isn't adapting quickly enough, and 98 percent say they need to overhaul their business model within the next three years. Smart leaders are looking for the next opportunity for growth and innovation.[1]

But the Deloitte "CFO Signals" report found that the Chief Financial Officers are not on board. Seventy-one percent said now is not a good time to take greater risks.[2] This is the paradox of change:

The status quo (however bad) feels *safer* than any imagined future might be *better*.

It's human nature to place your bets with what you know rather than risk it all on the promise of something better. Decades of research confirm this, and any team leader knows this in their gut. People resist change.

Great ideas will fail without a plan for the change.
Put another way, *innovation* cannot happen without a plan for the *people* who must change.

This book exists because strategic consulting is a $30 billion industry, but research suggests two-thirds of those well planned initiatives fail. *Leading Change*, John Kotter's seminal work in the field of change management, found that only 30 percent of change programs succeed. Similar studies in the decades since have reinforced this percentage.[3]

What's going on here? It boils down to the fact that companies are always paying for fresh new strategies that skim over the challenge of motivating teams to change. These strategies assume that once the "what" and "how" are clear, the "who" will be obvious and everyone affected by the change will willingly fall in line.

Most of the time the people who are expected to actually do the work to implement the change are left out of the planning. No one asks them about their needs, motivations, or expectations before planning for change. Sometimes, no one asks them at all.

Instead, senior leaders attend a "strategic offsite" to plan for the next year of objectives and key results (OKRs), then rush to announce the new direction at a company town hall or on the company intranet. Is it any wonder the rest of the company feels frustrated, fatigued, and resists any new changes?

COMMON PAIN POINTS

If you're tasked with leading any type of change or innovation in your organization, we're betting you've probably felt these pain points along the way:

— Your organization keeps investing in expensive strategy documents but none of them seem to ever get implemented successfully or stick around for very long.

— Especially when change is in the air, silos between teams become cemented into heavily guarded territories; teams resist sharing resources and information.

— Team members are just tired. There aren't many breakthrough creative ideas and willingness to pick up slack or volunteer goes way down.

Change is hard. Even tiny habits are hard to break. Anything that requires new processes, tools, or ways of working counts as change. All change is loss, and loss requires acknowledgement and time to resolve.

Pushing people to accept change and "just move on" often backfires. In the workplace this can look like defensiveness, "quiet quitting," or even active opposition.

WHAT MAKES PEOPLE WILLING TO CHANGE?

The opposite of resistance is *willingness*. Dr. Linda Hill, chair of the Leadership Initiative at Harvard Business School and co-author of *Collective Genius: The Art and Practice of Leading Innovation,* says people are willing to innovate when they are part of "a collaborative community bound by a compelling purpose."[4]

There's a lot packed into that short phrase.

— Does your team feel they were consulted on the change in a way that feels collaborative?

— Do they feel part of a community, bound by duty and care to support each other?

— Does the argument for the change compel them to move into that risky state of change and innovation?

— Do they agree with the larger purpose the organization is pursuing and the direction the leaders are taking?

Even if some of these areas are weak, a change leader may be able to use their authority to muscle a change into place. But launching a change is only the beginning. **Without collaboration, community, and a compelling purpose, don't expect change to stick.**

When the incentives (if incentives were even used at all), and the active accountability evaporate after the initial "push" is over, change will evaporate, too.

Innovations *launch* on passion, enthusiasm, good planning, and a vision for the future; innovations are *sustained* by a collaborative community bound by a compelling purpose.

If you want a team that is truly willing to change, you need to understand how they think, so you can help change how they feel, which will change what they can achieve.

BE THE LEADER THEY NEED

Without a doubt, you get it. You've got a team to motivate, a strategic plan in hand, a deadline looming, and you are simply too exhausted yourself to try and force, bribe, or drag your reluctant team to the finish line.

You need them to change, and do it willingly, but you also know that changing someone else's behavior can be an impossible task.

So let's focus on what you can control: your leadership efforts as you launch this change initiative. The best news? Many of the pitfalls and challenges to change are failures of planning, leadership, and communication. Those things are under your control.

Read on for the five ways that leaders sabotage change, areas you probably aren't even aware of that you can work on today.

FIVE WAYS LEADERS SABOTAGE CHANGE (AND WHAT TO DO ABOUT IT)

Even most well-meaning leaders can accidentally find themselves engaging in one of these self-sabotaging behaviors.

PITFALL NO. 1: THEY NARROWLY DEFINE THE PROBLEM.

Leaders are typically rewarded by achieving company goals and motivated by reducing the friction in their own job. But when leaders focus on company objectives or their own convenience over broader concerns, they sabotage their team by thinking too narrowly.

Unless the company engages in profit sharing and other team-based incentives, most team members just aren't motivated by helping the boss land their bonus or making their job easier. Individuals doing the work need to understand the "What's in it for me?" details. If they haven't personally experienced increased job satisfaction resulting from a change, or if they haven't heard compelling stories from other staff over a series of change initiatives, they are unlikely to believe that this next one will solve the right problems.

Zoom out, adapt, and refine your perspective.

Once you understand the problem from your team's point of view, you can adapt your solution to have the broadest benefit and therefore increase adoption. As you examine information from your team about the specific pros and cons of the proposed solutions, you should collaborate with them to adjust the change implementation details to meet those needs.

SOLUTION: SOLVE THE RIGHT PROBLEM. (CHAPTER ONE)

— Bring key people into the conversation early, listen to what they have to say, and develop a meaningful way to collect that information so that all stakeholders can review it.

— Use all the information to name the pain and locate the source.

— Determine what must happen and what can't happen by creating a Decision Framework.

— Brainstorm solutions broadly and refine options using the How/Now/Wow! Matrix.

— Choose a solution.

— Summarize and prioritize into a single, clear plan for change.

PITFALL NO. 2: THEY FORCE CHANGE. The "because I said so" style of change often comes from frustrated leaders who won't take the time to align goals (see above) and just want what they want. It can also come from a senior leader's mandate.

Either way, this heavy-handed approach removes autonomy and makes employees feel like children whose opinions and feedback aren't valued. In this case, the team may agree there is a problem, but in a rush or simply because they believe they know better, leaders select a solution and dictate how and how fast it will be implemented. Unfortunately, brute force, coercion, and even bribery are never well received, and they don't work long term. Change sticks when the team reframes the change as their own decision and believes in the same vision of success.

SOLUTION: SELL THE VISION. (CHAPTER TWO)

— Secure genuine sponsorship from executives and other staff with outsize influence by giving them a visible, important communication role.

— Build a Stakeholder Assessment Matrix.

— Track mindset change with Personas and Journey Maps.

— Facilitate confidential conversations to gather feedback and gauge resistance to the change initiative.

— Communicate about the perspectives you're hearing, the details of implementation, and how individuals can influence the remaining steps in the process. Rely on sponsors to help build support across the entire organization.

PITFALL NO. 3: THEY SILENCE RESISTANCE. When this sabotage is at play, leaders ask for feedback in situations where speaking up would feel uncomfortable or cost the employee social capital. This is the "We all agree, right?" approach.

Nodding heads or silence in an all-staff meeting does not equate to buy-in, but many leaders will accept this cursory "agreement" as permission and even enthusiasm to proceed. Then, when they find themselves mired in resistance as the initiative gets underway, leaders often express confusion. They truly felt they had the team's support. The end result is teams are left to fight it out about how the change will be implemented, or whether it will be abandoned.

SOLUTION: ADDRESS RESISTANCE AND POWER STRUGGLES. (CHAPTER THREE)

— Set an example for how to get ready for change.

— Calm "lizard brain" fears; then address rational resistance.

— Turn resistance into feedback you can use to improve the implementation plan.

— Share power whenever possible.

PITFALL NO. 4: THEY SHUFFLE PRIORITIES AND FAIL TO BUILD CAPACITY. This sabotage falls into the "ASAP" style of leading change. In this reactive leadership style, new work gets added to the top of the priority list without other items coming off the list, building in a permanent feeling of overwhelm and just asking for staff burnout. Assuming most teams are already fully booked with work, they don't have empty space just waiting to take on new initiatives. Plus, people take time to process change. Not only is it ineffective to rush the process without building capacity for ongoing, sustainable change, but rushing will also slow down the adoption of the change.

SOLUTION: BALANCE MOTIVATIONS AND WORKLOADS. (CHAPTER FOUR)

— Flex the solution to match team members' motivations by:

- identifying individual motivations.

- allocating tasks according to capabilities.

- uncovering and accounting for hidden work.

PITFALL NO. 5: THEY NEGLECT HEALTHY TEAM NORMS AND PSYCHOLOGICAL SAFETY. Are you investing *daily* in promoting healthy team norms and psychological safety? People are only willing to consider change when they feel part of a collaborative community bound by a compelling purpose. Leaders who don't invest time in creating a high-functioning team that welcomes feedback and rises to new challenges will find themselves lost when it comes to innovation and new initiatives.

Key questions to benchmark your team's psychological safety:

— Do team members speak openly and consider all perspectives?

— Is there a healthy attitude towards risk and failure?

— Are they genuinely willing to help each other reach shared goals?

— Do they collaborate and communicate efficiently or are they stuck in unproductive meetings for a majority of each day with no real time to do the work they feel they were hired to do?

SOLUTION: BUILD HEALTHY TEAM HABITS. (CHAPTER FIVE)

— Build psychological safety.

— Address broken team norms, including gaps in communication, collaboration and decision making.

— Define systems, processes, and workflows to promote effective meetings, communication (across all channels), and other work delivery.

— Address change fatigue and team uncertainty.

— Understand what is lost when a team doesn't have psychological safety or healthy team norms.

These are the five areas where leaders sabotage change, and they also happen to be the five steps leaders need both to launch a change and to sustain it—to make sure the change "sticks."

The rest of this book will take you through how to do that, right away. We want you to be able to read this book on a flight home from a conference where you just got excited about a new idea, so that you are ready with the tools you need once you're back in the office.

Let's get right to it.

01

SOLVE THE RIGHT PROBLEM

That study from AlixPartners referenced in the Introduction found that 85 percent of CEOs who say they want to "overhaul their business model" struggle to know where to start.[5]

Not surprising with such an ambitious goal that touches every part of a business. Most changes worth making touch multiple areas of the business and will have multiple impacts. So, how can you make sure your change efforts are focused in the right direction and intentionally designed to prevent change fatigue?

The first step is to get key stakeholders to align on the change, which involves not only agreeing to a proposed solution, but crucially, **agreeing that there is actually a problem worth solving.**

Many leaders skip straight to debating solutions. But it is crucial to make sure that everyone with valuable insights or who would be affected by the change actually agrees on the definition of the problem and the urgency around solving it.

That's why this chapter focuses not just on how to propose solutions, but on how to define the problem.

Defining the right problem is three-quarters of the solution.

What misalignment looks like in real life:

— The boss wants the team to start compiling more time-consuming reports when the team thinks the simpler ones work just fine or the boss isn't actually ever going to even look at the reports. (The team doesn't agree there is actually a problem worth the effort of solving.)

— The team agrees they need to collaborate more, but the leader's idea of a solution is more meetings. (The team doesn't believe meetings will fix the problem.)

— A small change, like agreeing on how to name documents to make them easier to find, that could make a big difference in team members' day-to-day work is not prioritized because leaders don't feel that frustration personally or the issue seems minor through the lens of productivity or output. (The leader doesn't think the problem is worth the time to fix.)

— Or your team needs to work with another team for the new initiative, but due to a lack of trust and communication, work breaks down into finger-pointing and blaming. (The teams don't trust each other enough to work together.)

As you can see, power dynamics often come into play when leaders decide which problems are worth fixing. But leaders who make these decisions without input risk alienating the very employees who make change possible. Leaders who want to innovate must treat everyone's frustrations as worthy of consideration, but often with mid-level managers in between, they are too far away from the action.

Gathering input is essential for defining the problem accurately as well giving the best chance for change to succeed. A compelling story that everyone agrees to is a key element of successful change.

Now, let's consider the work involved in ensuring everyone is clear on the definition and scope of the problem and agrees that the team is prepared and willing to do the work to address the root cause.

STEP
1:
Get the right people in the conversation

Often the issues that get addressed quickly are pain points for people at the top of the organizational hierarchy, because that's where the strategy team and decision makers sit.

It's important not to overrepresent those with power and importance in the organization, because fixing a small issue felt by dozens of people can be just as significant as addressing a top-tier crisis. And solving minor problems continuously for the broader team builds goodwill for future initiatives that may have less measurable "What's in it for me?" benefits to individuals.

So how do leaders ensure they are asking the right questions to determine the right problems to solve? **When considering how to address strategic challenges, they bring in perspectives from**

throughout the organization. They consider who in the organization—no matter who they report to—might have ideas about all the ways to achieve the same goal.

For example, multiple organizations we've advised have faced the specific problem of duplicated effort and wasted resources when building graphics and creative assets. In these cases, due to growth, individual teams hired their own creative talent or outsourced their creative projects to an agency partner that works only with their team, instead of having a centralized "shared services" model.

Leaders in these organizations wondered if creative talent would be more effective if they were to collaborate on projects, build more visually unified creative assets, and prevent duplication of effort. To answer this question, they went on a "listening tour," consulting with:

— department leaders who were used to having their own creative team without having to share resources. (E.g., managers overseeing this work who might feel their power shift as their team's responsibilities change.)

— the people doing the work whose roles might evolve—the creative designers, writers, and producers who were used to working for a single department.

— the finance and procurement teams who could attest to the budget implications.

— long-tenured staff who had observed this problem for a while and had witnessed other attempted solutions.

In these situations, the leaders used these interviews to weigh the pros and cons of leaving things the same or exploring a solution. As they validated their concern with a smaller group, they then took findings back to a strategic planning team, and finally circulated a written problem statement to a wider group of people who would have an opinion on the effectiveness of the current team structure.

Listening earns you credibility, which earns you respect, which earns you influence.

This cascading of the problem to a broader group uncovers any dependencies or risks and helps promote initial awareness of the problem with key stakeholders. It is valuable at the early stages to include anyone who might be there at the implementation. Who (and how) you include in the next few steps will vary based on your team culture, the specific challenge you're facing, the size of the problem, and the timeline for change.

Being willing to pause and engage with staff during the problem-definition process is essential to secure buy-in for any related change process. All too often, leaders responsible for getting things done are so busy chipping away at specific objectives and key results they forget to intentionally recognize their workers' power and areas of control. Or they feel as though letting staff see the messy process of problem solving would diminish trust or show that the leaders don't have it all figured out. This closed-door approach leaves employees feeling left out and dictated to instead of included and collaborative.

When employees feel they have not been consulted, they tend to double down on the things they can control, which exacerbates "office politics," back-channel discussions and impulses to grow territorial on one end of the spectrum, or disengagement from the success of the company on the other end.

The best way to avoid this issue is to consider with empathy how expressing your concerns will be perceived. It is a fine balance between healthy transparency and oversharing every frustration. To get buy-in, you need to engage honestly about what needs to change, but you must do so in a way that doesn't make your team feel overly criticized or lead them to respond defensively or proactively start to protect their jobs.

Once the change initiative kicks off formally, your team members will have many questions that boil down to "how does this affect me?" Here, the problem-definition phase, is where you can prepare to answer those questions.

Bring broad and diverse perspectives. People will do almost anything to avoid feeling powerless. Even if the change is not optional and there is very little room for feedback to change the outcome, it's important to open the floor to them, hear the comments, and consider even minor flexibility that can be accommodated. When team members at every level feel included, and effort is made to ensure everyone agrees on the problem, silos disappear, motivation improves, entrepreneurial thinking abounds as everyone collaborates on a solution.

Acknowledging diverse opinions and inviting active participation in problem-definition sessions also helps underscore how valuable team members are in major changes. From an employee engagement perspective, this can help employees feel heard and recognized, which makes it more likely they will feel intrinsically motivated to participate in the change, rather than dictated to. In fact, creating meaning is an important part of driving employee engagement.

Another benefit of acknowledging more opinions from diverse sources is that sometimes the best input comes from insightful individuals who won't be directly affected but have enough experience to predict how the team might respond and point out areas to consider. As Adam Grant shared in his book *Think Again*, "We want people with dissimilar traits and backgrounds but similar principles."

When you invite diverse ways of thinking, you can help drive new ideas; shared values help support collaboration. Bringing in more voices also helps reduce the impact of the biases everyone brings to decision making, including:

— **confirmation bias.** People interpret what they see based on what they already believe.

— **participation bias.** People react based on how they think they're expected to react.

— **consistency bias.** People think their opinion now was the same as their opinion in the past.

— **desirability bias.** People see what they want to see.

These biases can create blind spots in our thinking and lead us to the wrong decisions.[6] Inviting others to weigh in early can help decision makers avoid unintended consequences. As you, the change leader, consider how broadly to circulate the challenge statement for feedback, think about the experiences each participant brings in addition to their background. Invite people who may be skeptical to challenge.

STEP

2:

AGREE ON A PROBLEM STATEMENT

Once you identify who to consult on the challenge as outlined in Step One, it's time to make sure you ask the right questions. *What isn't working? What are the symptoms? Who is feeling the pain?*

The next goal is to name the actual problem and figure out what the team is willing to invest to solve it.

So how exactly do you do this? Start by having a brainstorm session with a representative subset of the broad group you identified above who can help you get specific, and pressure test the contributing factors to the problem you've identified. It's important at this phase to focus exclusively on the problem, without driving towards a proposed solution.

Write a detailed description of the problem and share it with individuals throughout the organization that are impacted by (or contribute to) the challenge.

Depending on the openness and psychological safety of your team culture (see Chapter Five if you're not sure!), this may be an easygoing exchange or a guarded one. For teams with difficulty sharing openly, a change facilitator can be an excellent neutral third party at this stage, as can an anonymous feedback method for employees to weigh in without consequences.

Thoughtful facilitation of this discussion is required to allow for different voices of the team to be heard. Take the time to understand the conditions of the problem to understand its scope.

Consider the root cause. Although you may start with a problem statement, you may still need to zoom out even further to ensure you are getting to the core of the problem, not just symptoms.

At the start of this book, we met "Bianca," who could take steps to make her job easier by asking project owners to keep their project information updated in a shared database rather than collect it painfully each month. Why does she resist?

In this example, the project owners had historically viewed each other as competitors, and didn't like to share details with their counterparts. They were OK sharing the status with Bianca directly each month, but entering real-time data in a shared system where anyone could track their progress? No way.

In this case the symptom her boss was trying to solve was about data collection and efficiency, but underneath there was a culture problem that would keep even the most rational solution from succeeding. The proposed solution didn't address the root cause, Bianca knew it, and resisted making the effort she knew would fail.

This is why it is so important to understand the root cause of the issue: to design a solution that is more likely to solve the problem permanently and have sustained adoption. Limited resources require comprehensive solutions that don't just fight symptoms or make us feel good for doing something.

Often the pain point that starts the change discussion is actually part of a larger issue or linked to other challenges. The team needs to decide whether to address the big picture or solve the smaller issues one at a time.

How This Works in the Real World

As a result of a departmental restructure, one team we worked with said they were struggling with project management and prioritizing work in the new structure. Each team was used to working as an independent group with limited collaboration and a lot of autonomy. In talking with team members, we discovered that the problem wasn't project management, but was a result of uncertainty about shared responsibilities and general feelings of resentment about losing that autonomy. Through a series of workshops, we were able to help team members address the "elephant in the room" (the unspoken feelings and beliefs) to define new ways of working based on the new structure. **The root cause was the changing power dynamics, not the symptomatic issue of project management and task deadlines.**

You may find it too difficult to call out the root cause. Maybe the root cause is part of the CEO's deeply held beliefs or a complicated, embedded process. It may only be possible to try to come up with solutions that don't "rock the boat" too much and address only a symptom or two.

More often than not, leaders may take a business-focused view of change and fail to think about consequences for the end user or their customer.

Just a warning that this type of problem-solving can bring long-term change fatigue, making the whole process harder than just doing the tough work up front. It is the equivalent of cutting off one head of the Hydra just to have another grow in its place. In an ideal world, the solution addresses the root cause.

On the other hand, we understand that sometimes teams have to settle for symptom relief. Even if you can't address the full root cause, it is useful to have a grasp of the bigger picture to help with future planning. Team member interviews or surveys provide details around the feeling of "something's not right." With this information, you can use a deeper root cause analysis to help you get to the heart of the problem.

Use the "Five Whys Exercise" to uncover the root cause. One helpful exercise to get at the root cause is called the "Five Whys" exercise. Let's say an organization has deep departmental silos and information is not flowing between them. This results in various teams paying different vendors for the same customer research and not sharing results. A rushed and ineffective solution might call for all projects to run through a complicated procurement process to ensure no overlap, but the Five Whys exercise will uncover a better solution that gets at the root cause. Here's an example.

Pain: We're paying multiple vendors to interview our customers and define their wants/needs.

1. Why? Because each team has slightly different questions they want to ask.

2. Why? Because their leadership hasn't aligned on goals.

3. Why? Because they each have their own research budgets and autonomy.

4. Why? Because department leaders feel they have more power and control if they manage their projects independently.

5. Why? Because the organization hasn't aligned incentives across teams to give up some autonomy and power in return for other rewards.

Possible better solution: Bring leaders to the table to build a Center of Excellence on audience insights. Use the overlapping vendor budgets to build tools and processes that make contributing and accessing information easy. Visibly reward information sharing and collaboration.

As you finalize your problem statement and confirm the root cause, you'll observe that there is an emotional side to the issue, not just the rational, data-driven problem.

Generally speaking, people don't behave rationally: they believe they use facts and logic to choose the best solution, but behavioral scientists and economists tell us that the prefrontal cortex, the part of the brain considered to be the decision-maker, is actually not in charge.

As behavioral designer Robin Kriglstein says, "All conscious behavior is driven by emotion."[7] Humans aren't really persuaded by data, and if we're only defining the problem in terms of data then we're missing a huge opportunity. Humans make decisions both rationally and emotionally, but often leaders use arguments for change that overly emphasize the rational, which can lead to resistance that leaders can find baffling. We'll talk more about how neuroscience impacts decision making and resistance in Chapter Three.

At this point, you're trying to achieve strategic alignment and awareness. Leaders need to:

— showcase what they're trying to achieve, clearly, concretely, with metrics.

— consider all the aspects of the pain as the team agrees on what's worth addressing.

— get people aligned on the urgent need to solve this particular problem.

Once you have what feels like a solid problem statement, it's time to prepare for finding the perfect-fit solution. During the next stage, you will further refine the initial thinking and create an actionable guide for your solution stage.

STEP
3:
CREATE A DECISION FRAMEWORK

Once you've identified the right problem to solve, it's tempting to jump right into brainstorming solutions. If you do that, you'll be skipping a crucial step that helps you define success: a decision framework.

A decision framework is simply the criteria (what must happen) and constraints (what can't happen) that the team uses to determine whether a given solution will be a good fit. Decision frameworks intentionally define shared requirements, context, and constraints to support high-quality decisions.

For example, if you were considering buying a house, you need to identify your budget and geography (constraints) as well as your wish list of features like number of bathrooms and a cool kitchen (criteria) before you start browsing online real estate listings for new digs. Constraints and criteria are critical inputs in problem solving.

The key value in building a decision framework is making your brainstorm more efficient. If the team understands exactly how the problem is defined, as well as the "must do/can't do" elements (criteria/constraints), the ideas coming from the brainstorm are more likely to be a good match for the problem.

It's important to agree on the decision framework before any actual solutions are brainstormed. This agreement is the difference between daydreaming and planning. Busy leaders do NOT have time for unrealistic solutions. Here's how to create a decision framework to make sure that the focus stays on workable ideas.

Label constraints and criteria. To begin building a decision framework, start by listing known constraints. When it comes to assessing a problem, constraints often follow in one of these three buckets.

— **Scope:** What is the work required to solve the problem? Are there certain team members whose time is required to make this a success? Who needs to approve?

— **Timing:** Does the problem have to be solved by a certain time? How long will it take and does a longer or shorter runway need to be considered?

— **Budget:** How much money can be invested to meet our objective?

List all the constraints first. From there, it's time to brainstorm criteria, aka your wish list. It's OK if this list is too long or it seems like no solution could possibly meet the criteria. Withhold judgment for now.

Do not begin evaluating and comparing solutions until *everyone who might have the power to sandbag this project:*

— agrees on the problem. (If not, go back to Step Two in this chapter.)

— weighs in on the "wish list" criteria for solutions.

— contributes a workable idea to the set of possible solutions or votes for someone else's proposed solution.

How This Works in the Real World

Let's go back to the problem of the team not being able to find the documents and files they need. When we worked with this company, one idea to solve the problem was to invest more than $250,000 to set up a new knowledge management system (with an additional $100,000 fee each year). Another idea was to extensively train people on things like file names and folder structure so that everyone used the same conventions consistently. In this case, the team had to agree on whether budget or time is the more significant constraint in the brainstorming process.

How do you decide which one matters more? More importantly, how do you decide this as a group? In our real-world example, the team chose to invest in the new tool due to a culture of resistance to change and extra process, they chose to implement the tool.

If the executives at your company are firmly on the side of spending no money and the team members are firmly on the side of protecting their time, the solution process is at an impasse. Who will decide what matters more? What if there are multiple factors to consider?

One of the best ways to evaluate subjective ideas is with a framework designed by the team. It's hard for people to argue with the results when they helped build the rubric.

Pairwise Comparison is a research technique that helps identify priorities and rank a list of items by comparing them two at a time. You compare every item on your wish list to every other item. The result is a weight for each criterion that you can apply to your decision framework.

Take a look at the chart. This is the list of criteria for the team with the "can't-find-anything-we-need" problem. In the left column, they listed all the criteria that mattered: effort to set up, ease of ongoing use, initial cost, ongoing cost, and technical support required from the IT team.

PAIRWISE COMPARISON CHART

CRITERIA	SETUP EFFORT (A)	EASY TO USE (B)	SETUP COST (C)	ANNUAL COST (D)	IT SUPPORT (E)	TOTAL VOTES	CRITERIA WEIGHT
SETUP EFFORT (A)		B	C	D	E	0	0%
EASY TO USE (B)			B	B	B	4	40%
SETUP COST (C)				DC	C	2	20%
ANNUAL COST (D)					D	3	30%
IT SUPPORT (E)						1	10%
						10	100%

compare A to B
and put winner in the box
if it's a tie, put both.

In Pairwise comparison, each criterion is compared to every other. If there's a tie, they both go in the box. Then total the votes for each criteria item across *the entire chart*.

You can see that "Easy to Use" won the Pairwise Comparison *four times*, where Ongoing IT Support only won one time. The criterion of ease of use is not just more important, but it is four times more important. Later when ranking solutions, the weighted percentage can provide more insight into which option is truly the best fit.

Once you've created the decision framework, you will use it to help you rank solutions after the brainstorming process in Step Four.

Define success metrics. Especially when solving complex problems, it's important to define the ideal end state and how you will measure success. What will indicate that the problem is resolved? Many leaders look for data points they can see on a dashboard. *E.g., Are people logging into the new knowledge management tool?* But qualitative metrics like employee satisfaction with the solution can be even more supportive of the long-term sustainability of your initiative. Include in your decision framework some "soft metrics" like how easy it is to use the new tool. This ensures that the cheaper option doesn't always win, at the expense of employee satisfaction.

Stick with the process. The trick is not to declare yourself done with this step until everyone who could impact the success of the solution joins the quest. **Any project that attempts to move forward with key influencers unwilling or unable to even agree on the problem is on shaky ground from the very beginning.**

► MILESTONE ACHIEVED

Problem Defined

Now is a great moment to communicate a major milestone to your stakeholders. You've done the work to define the problem in a way that your entire team can understand, included them in the assessment of the problem and given them a powerful story about why this problem is worth their time, right now.

On to the solution!

STEP
4:
BRAINSTORM
SOLUTIONS

Now that the team all agrees that there is a problem, and the team all agrees on what must happen and what can't happen in our ideal new future, it's time to brainstorm!

By this point in the process, some teams we've worked with have designated a working group to move forward with a subset of highly invested team members that have the trust of the others in the organization. Other teams prefer to keep brainstorming and solution selection broad, ensuring every voice has equal weight. One approach prioritizes efficiency, one prioritizes inclusivity. Selecting the approach can highly impact your success, so think carefully about who to include as this process unfolds.

The team needs to dream about what could be, within the limits of our decision framework. At the start of the initial discussion, make sure you set expectations about the outcomes of the session to ensure the vision and purpose is clear. Clarify the premise, the team's role in the discussion, and the definition of success to shape the ideas and action items coming out of your session. Dreaming works best when the basic rules of brainstorming are followed.[8]

Explore ALL possible routes. Take ideas from EVERYWHERE. Give *everyone at every level* the opportunity to propose solutions that meet the criteria. Share the problem definition and decision framework widely and recruit ideas in many channels: anonymous idea box, team meetings, creative jam sessions, etc.

Often when considering options for solutions, human brains will naturally look for ways to point out the flaws in the idea, but this can artificially limit what is possible. According to Roger L. Martin's book, *A Better Way to Think*, guide your brainstorming team to take a "possibility-based approach" instead, asking how to use constraints to help generate new ideas. Use the prompt, "How might we..." to brainstorm new options. For example, "How might we use our existing software in a new way to make files easier to find without buying a new system?"

Defer judgment and ruthlessly unearth hidden assumptions. Ignore how the solution "should" look. Make sure you're not dismissing one option too early. Avoid black and white decision thinking. There are always more options, and alternate paths to the same outcome. What do you think you know? Are you sure? Many, many times we've encountered teams with firm assumptions they are building their entire strategies around. *"They'll never let us buy a tool." "We can't outsource that." "She'd never go for that idea."* These assumptions turn out time and again to be completely false and hold back the company's growth.

Encourage wild ideas. When someone suggests a completely wild idea that meets the criteria, one of two things might happen; either the team accepts that this solution should be considered *or* it's a good catch that a constraint was missed that would have eliminated this particular solution.

Revisit criteria as needed (with some healthy debate!) until you have a list of decent solutions that meet the agreed upon criteria.

Build on the ideas of others. Invite cooperation into the brainstorm. Many ideas get better with discussion because the teams can't always identify the assumptions and limitations they are bringing to the brainstorm. Encourage small group discussions about the problem and potential solutions. Hearing another person describe the problem from another perspective is sometimes all it takes to open up a whole new category of solutions.

You completed the previous steps of solving the right problem and creating a decision framework to help the team stay focused on the problem at hand. It is impossible to fix everything, and therefore important to identify what problems are off the table for this exercise.

If the challenge at hand is a large one, consider phased solutions that allow the team to "eat the elephant one bite at a time" and learn from each phase, rather than trying to craft a solution that perfectly and comprehensively addresses all pain points. A phased approach also is often a more actionable way to show some positive impact with a minimum amount of effort, and also gain momentum by doing the small thing successfully.

Go for quantity. More is better. The eventual best solution will likely be a combination of multiple ideas. Keeping a large quantity of ideas on the table at the beginning will ensure plenty of ingredients in the final recipe for change. This phase is considered *divergent thinking*, where the team broadens their thinking to consider lots of options. The next phase of refinement is the *convergent thinking* step where options are reduced down to a workable few.

Often when balancing the needs of different stakeholder groups, consistency for its own sake can come into play. ("If team A gets a resource, then we need one too.") It's important that the impacts to each group are considered to ensure the intended outcomes are realized. Watch out for prioritizing an idea too soon and adapting per each group requirement.

Refine options. Brainstorming is an example of expansive thinking: more is better. The next step is to sort the pile of ideas into something workable—narrowing it down to a few ideas to evaluate.

As the brainstorming wraps up, the team that generated all these ideas needs to begin weeding some out, leaving only the most feasible recommendations to carry forward in the process or take to the decision-makers. Consider using the *Gamestorming* How-Now-Wow matrix to narrow down the possible solutions.[9] In the exercise, teams work together to evaluate each idea for how difficult or easy it will be to implement, and on the originality of the idea.

HOW/NOW/WOW MATRIX

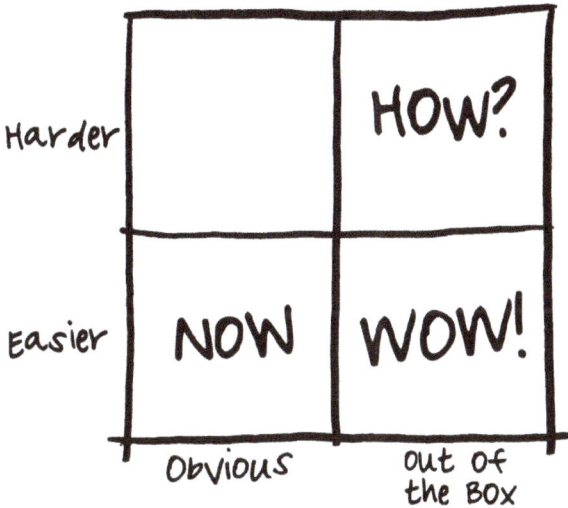

- Innovative, breakthrough ideas that are not that hard to implement are "WOW!" ideas.

- Ideas that are pretty easy but not that innovative fall into the "NOW" bucket: easy, low risk, and unlikely to rock the boat or require major change.

- Put ideas that are very innovative but also pretty tough to implement in the "HOW?" bucket for evaluation as part of your long-term strategic planning.

STEP
5:
CHOOSE A SOLUTION

When evaluating your proposed solutions, it's important to remember that the best plans account for PROCESS, PURPOSE and PEOPLE. They don't just solve the problem at hand, they solve the unspoken problem, they account for the new problems that change will create, and they are thoughtful enough to be trustworthy to those you are asking to change.

At this point, most teams are pretty clear on which solutions they want to consider.

A useful exercise to continue pressure testing these proposed solutions is to consider who each proposed solution would impact, assign the brainstorming team a corresponding role, and role-play how this solution would be received.

How This Works in the Real World

In the previous example about considering a unified knowledge management tool, the brainstorming team suggested that the organization move away from a messy Google Drive system for sharing documents and instead purchase a dedicated knowledge management system to organize files. They drew names to role-play how that proposal might be received by IT, Legal, Finance, Executive teams, and various departments. This helped to uncover questions and concerns that needed to be addressed and could have derailed this tool as a possible solution.

Consider the "do-ability." It's time to think about any constraints to evaluate what needs to be removed from the list of ideas. Consider the skills and abilities of team members who will be driving the change. Look at dependencies across the organization and other projects that may impact your upcoming work.

It can also make sense to identify any headwinds and tailwinds the team may encounter as they implement this change. There may be a clear winner of a solution but if outside forces could make it harder, the team may want to consider a second-choice solution with an easier path to implementation.

For example, if adding a new feature to the product might alienate your biggest customers, their approval acts as an "outside force" pushing against the new feature. Or, as interest rates rise companies may become more risk averse and choose to postpone change initiatives or new hires until things feel more stable. Macroeconomic forces make the solution more difficult.

Gauge the difficulty. The same team that has been brainstorming and evaluating ideas should now consider what forces are driving and resisting change, both internal and external. A useful tool is the Force Field Analysis, a framework developed in the 1940s in social science research and popularized by *Gamestorming*.[10] [11]

How This Works in the Real World

We worked with a client that was considering a change initiative to move all creative functions onto the same team. At the time, each department had a graphic designer working on department-specific materials. As the organization grew, this led to some skills being overrepresented and other skills missing from the organization. In addition, designers frequently were doing work that was the same or very similar to work that had already been done in another department.

Centralizing the function would increase efficiency, collaboration, and speed of projects getting done (represented in the FOR column on the left). Working against the change is the corporate culture of department autonomy, the different tools and processes each designer is used to, and the complicated H.R. mess that a reorganization of reporting relationships would entail.

FORCE FIELD ANALYSIS

Once the team identified key forces working for and against the centralization, each force was assigned a score for each force from 1 (weak) to 5 (strong), and we totaled the scores on each side to evaluate the difficulty of implementing this change in the face of these forces. This team decided that the time wasn't right for a full centralization as there were a number of critical projects keeping the various designers busy and asking them to make a big change would be poorly received.

Instead, an alternate plan to formalize project sharing and awareness of what other teams were doing was implemented to enhance collaboration in advance of a potential future centralization of the work.

Host an "Idea Deathmatch." If your team is still having trouble agreeing on a solution, you can enhance the Pairwise Comparison exercise above in what we refer to as an "Idea Deathmatch" to more explicitly weigh criteria and compare potential solutions. *(Step-by-step instructions can be found at* changefatigue.com.*)*

Keep at it until you have a solution that the team agrees is important, urgent, and doable. Then pause and pat yourself on the back because the work you've done up to this point is setting your team up for a much easier change initiative.

▶ MILESTONE ACHIEVED

Solution Proposed

Congratulations! You've chosen the change!

STEP
6:
SUMMARIZE AND PRIORITIZE

Now is the time to distill all that effort you put into defining a solution into a single, clear plan for change with milestones and a timeline as you prepare to Sell the Vision in Chapter Two.

Here's an example of a single slide outlining a change:

CHANGE SUMMARY SLIDE

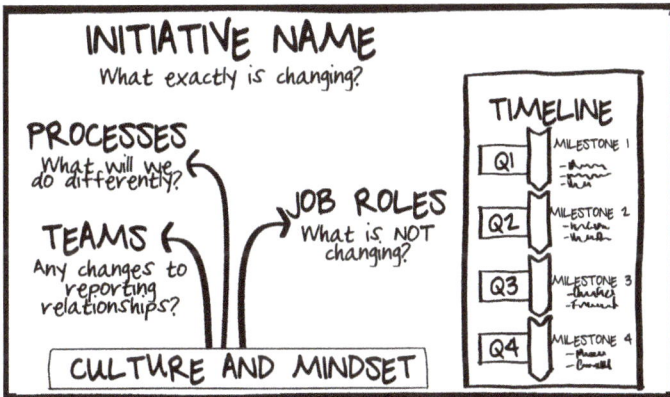

(Visit changefatigue.com for a this and other templates)

At the top of the slide, outline WHAT is changing, as briefly as possible. In succinct bullets, describe one to two benefits to the organization as a whole and specific job roles that will see benefits like workload reduction or increase efficiency. Use the main portion of the slide to cover what they can expect in the four main areas of change:

— Process changes

  - What will be done differently?

  - What is not changing?

— Organizational structure

  - Any changes to reporting relationships?

  - Who is leading the change?

— Role changes

  - Who will be responsible for the new work activities?

— Culture and mindsets

  - What changes to culture and mindsets will need to be embraced?

Be sure to include major milestones along the way and a rough estimate for when each milestone will be achieved.

At this point, you're ready to share the vision for the change with others. It can be a great way to confirm understanding with an executive team in advance of sharing it with others.

This step is called "summarize and prioritize" because we can almost guarantee that your solution has too much packed into the plan. **If you are struggling to figure out how to get everything from your solution into a single slide that likely means you have a phased change to consider.**

A broad timeline of activities may help you communicate the key considerations and prioritize where you plan to explore further. You can use a "Now, Next, Future" matrix to help frame future discussions.

Think about the big categories of work that will drive the change. Chunk these categories into milestones, identify the team members that will complete the work and schedule work based on your project requirements. The graphic below shows an example for how to organize this.

NOW/NEXT/FUTURE PLANNING

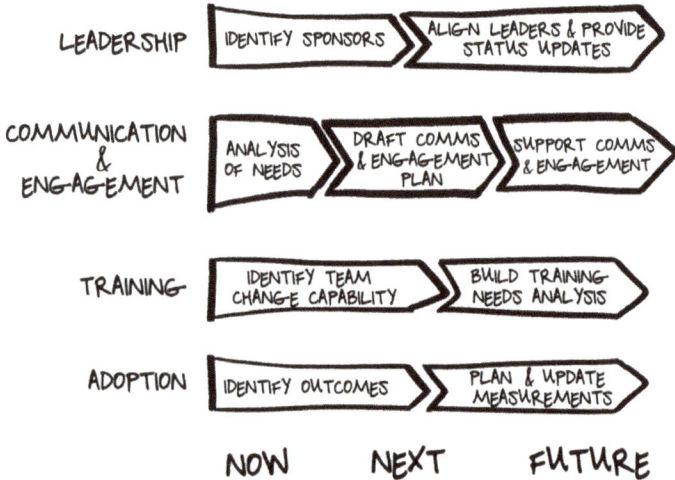

LEADERSHIP

IDENTIFY SPONSORS → ALIGN LEADERS & PROVIDE STATUS UPDATES

COMMUNICATION & ENGAGEMENT

ANALYSIS OF NEEDS → DRAFT COMMS & ENGAGEMENT PLAN → SUPPORT COMMS & ENGAGEMENT

TRAINING

IDENTIFY TEAM CHANGE CAPABILITY → BUILD TRAINING NEEDS ANALYSIS

ADOPTION

IDENTIFY OUTCOMES → PLAN & UPDATE MEASUREMENTS

NOW   NEXT   FUTURE

What are the first four to five milestones that need to be accomplished?

Limit your summary to those four or five milestones and create a slide for each of the various phases. Most of the time, each phase requires different individuals to provide time and input anyway, so the change makes sense to split up into phases. A single slide summarizing each phase as a milestone can be a helpful overview for leadership or project organizers.

Before you go further, consider staffing gaps. Many projects we've worked on make it to this point and realize they're going to need some help. There are a number of ways teams can add resources, depending on the nature of the change. Sometimes a new hire in a specific department dedicated to the new initiative is needed. More often the proposed idea requires a little bit of change across lots of people throughout the organization, with some teams or individuals affected more than others.

02

SELL THE VISION

In Chapter One, you as the change leader identified the problem to be solved, evaluated a solution, and engaged with key team members to help make those assessments along the way.

Now it's time to move from deciding *what* to do to determining *who* will do the work and *how* it's going to get done. Let's spend some time identifying the people who will impact the success of this initiative.

UNDERSTAND YOUR STAKEHOLDERS

Now that you've outlined the problem and summarized a proposed solution at a high level, it's time to turn your attention to assessing your stakeholders. As we defined at the outset, your **stakeholders are the people who will be impacted by the change in any way, on any level.** Stakeholders can make or break your initiative, depending on their enthusiasm, their resistance, and the impact of their influence.

No project succeeds without winning over key stakeholders. You've already begun that work by reaching out to them to make sure they agree the change addresses a problem worth solving. (We shared guidelines for how to do this in Chapter One.)

Now, it's time to further differentiate between the stakeholders involved in your change. Some stakeholders will be part of the entire process.

SELL THE VISION

Others will act as guardrails, only piping up or joining the process when their particular expertise is required. (Legal, finance, and I.T. team members often fit in this bucket.)

From here we'll begin our Stakeholder Assessment Matrix.

Draft a Stakeholder Assessment Matrix (SAM). A SAM gives you a holistic view of who to consider throughout the change journey. It will be the foundation to drive and build sponsorship, communication and training plans for different groups through different parts of the change journey. The SAM becomes a master list of key team members who will be impacted or can influence a project. (*Download the Stakeholder Assessment Matrix template at* <u>changefatigue.com</u>.)

At its most basic, the SAM is a spreadsheet with each stakeholder's name and team or department in the first columns followed by four basic assessments.

1. What is their **ROLE** in the change? (E.g., sponsor, an impacted leader, a senior manager, a change champion, a super user, an influencer, etc.)

2. What is their **ATTENTION** level? Are they eagerly awaiting updates on this project or waiting to see if it will impact their role?

3. What is their **MINDSET,** their level of support for the initiative? (E.g., early adopter, neutral, disinterested, active resister, etc.)

4. How much **PULL** do they have? What is their ability to impact or influence the outcome of the initiative?

Who should be included in an SAM? A Stakeholder Assessment should include anyone impacted by the change, and that list is likely longer than just the individuals who will have new tasks in their role. Make a list of everyone who can impact the success of the project, regardless of where they sit in the company hierarchy. Start with executives and decision-makers, add in the obvious (and not-so-obvious) individuals whose approval or vote of confidence will help your initiative succeed, and of course, the impacted end users.

Your early drafts of your SAM will likely feature the most obvious individuals necessary for the change to succeed. As you refine the details of the change initiative, you'll cast a wider net.

Don't forget people who may not be obviously impacted but have lots of influence, like staff who have been with the organization for a long time or the ones who hold the budget or hiring decisions. Impacted team members will look to stakeholders in power seats to decide how eagerly to adopt the change, so their approval can be a vital boost to your project.

Some key questions to ask as you consider who to list in your Stakeholder Assessment:

— Who is going to have to do their job differently?

— Who will need new training, resources, or support?

— Who will lose resources or support as a result of this change?

— Who might resist or speak out against this change?

— Who could delay or cancel the whole project?

— Who needs to approve or feel like they were consulted?

— Who gets to define success?

— Who will get credit for the success?

There are several aspects of a person's job that can change, such as how their job performance is measured and rewarded, who they work with, and more.

WORK DELIVERY
• STRATEGIC THINKING (WHAT)
• STRATEGIC PLANNING (HOW)
• LOCATION

WORKFLOW PROCESS
• TOOLS
• SYSTEMS
• INFORMATION FLOW

WHAT MIGHT CHANGE WITH A CHANGE?

JOB PERFORMANCE
• ROLES
• $$ COMPENSATION
• JOB DESCRIPTION

WAYS OF WORKING
• PRINCIPLES
• PERSPECTIVE
• BEHAVIORS

RELATIONSHIPS
• INTERNAL TEAM OR SQUAD
• REPORTING
• CUSTOMERS

Building a SAM often starts with a list of all the staff, and then a removal of any names that are not impacted in any way. Then a RAMP categorization (defining the **role, attention, mindset,** and **pull)** will help identify key stakeholders that need custom communications.

For example, if an organization is considering a new Intranet to help keep track of things like H.R. documents, payroll documents, and internal policies, the roles might be:

— **Intranet Publishers:** H.R. and department leaders that add most of the content to the Intranet.

— **I.T.:** The technical team that will set up and maintain the actual platform, upgrades, content migration, etc.

- **Executives and Finance:** Organizational leaders who likely won't use the system much but need to understand the basic function and value to lend their support.

- **Managers:** These folks need to know how to train their team to use the Intranet instead of asking questions to find relevant information.

- **Staff and Users:** This is the bulk of the organization, those with little impact on how the system gets set up but the most day-to-day usage. Their satisfaction will be essential to long term adoption, even if they don't have much power in the setup process.

Within each of these roles there will be various **mindsets** that individuals bring to the change. Here are a few.

- **Promoter** is someone involved and invested in the success of the change. They know the ins and outs and can answer questions, and they are trying to accrue support.

- **Potential Sponsor** is available for high-level updates and believe in the project but are not available or interested in becoming a promoter.

- **Skeptic** doesn't trust the argument for change, OR the messenger, (or possibly both). They are waiting and seeing.

- **Apathetic** is someone who doesn't mind going along with the change unless it starts to take resources away from their projects or impact their work.

— **Resister** opposes the change, whether vocally or quietly.

Identifying **pull** and **attention** are often intuitive, quick assessments. *How much does this person's opinion matter in the big picture? How likely are they to give the change serious attention to help it succeed?*

Use the Influence and Interest Matrix. When determining who should be involved in collaborating to support a successful implementation, it's important to consider availability, interest in the project, and their influence in the organization.

The Influence and Interest Matrix is a helpful tool to identify the right individuals. This will also be useful in later stages of the process as you identify supporters, detractors, and leadership sponsors.

INFLUENCE & INTEREST MATRIX

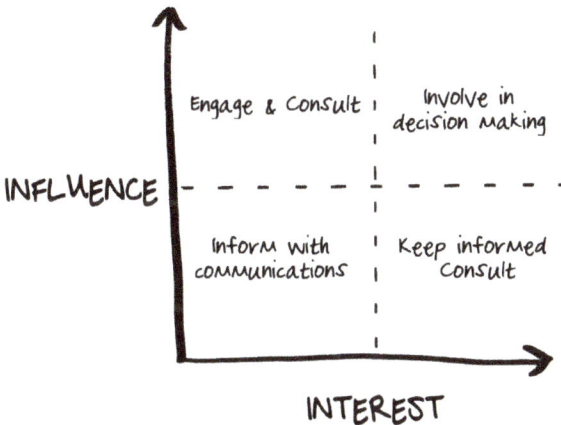

INFLUENCE

Engage & Consult

Involve in decision making

Inform with communications

Keep informed Consult

INTEREST

RECRUIT AND RALLY SPONSORS

Throughout all the phases of the change, leaders from different parts of the organization will need to use their own social capital and communication channels to support the initiative. Sponsors may be senior executives who have limited day-to-day involvement in the project, respected staff who serve as mentors or have long experience with the organization's history, or influential members and managers from the teams most impacted by the change.

Essentially, anyone who will be asked about the initiative needs to be equipped to explain and show their support for the change. Take a look at the Influence/Interest graphic above. Individuals who are high on both scales make excellent candidates for active sponsorship.

Active, visible sponsors play a critical role in the success of your initiative. According to Prosci's 20th Annual "Best Practices in Change Management" report, **"Projects with an extremely effective sponsor met or exceeded objectives more than twice as often as those with a very ineffective sponsor."**[12]

In change initiatives that don't have an intentional strategy to identify sponsors, the answer to "Who is leading the change?" is often a low-power project manager or the person responsible for implementation.

Successful initiatives engage influential sponsors who want the change to succeed and know the valuable role they play. Successful change needs these top-down sponsors in addition to the stakeholders you've tapped to help define the problem and draft the change initiative. **Key activities for sponsors:**

— Stay informed on major developments and delivery requirements to be prepared to answer at least general questions and redirect others to initiative leaders.

— Use social capital to engage across the organization to promote the change.

— Share communications about the initiative from their owned channels (e.g., email, employee announcements) and participate in change activities.

— Role-model participation and encourage other leaders and managers to participate and support the change.

— Where applicable, encourage executive or board support.

"During change, leadership provides a psychological focal point for followers by offering a role model who demonstrates desired actions."

—Ann-Louise Holten

Also consider availability. Many leaders are faced with multiple requests to support initiatives. Think about how available the potential sponsor is to drive the change. Teams dread the "ghost" sponsor, the leader that shows up for the kickoff, then disappears. Or worse, a sponsor that doesn't believe in the change.

Make sure you have identified the right level of sponsor who has credibility in supporting the change. They can help uncover issues the initiative may need to address and prevent confusion around resource requirements and priorities. In the end, this can reduce program delays and boost visibility with the right people identified to support change efforts.

Select change sponsors to recruit. Think about the following criteria for change sponsorship.

— Does the sponsor have formal authority or specific delegated authority to lead the change?
— Do they have the credibility to be an effective sponsor?
— Will they offer support and remove any blockers to the program efforts?
— Have they been involved in successful change initiatives in the past?
— Do they understand the change and are they willing to show active support?

Once you identify this group, begin communicating about the change initiative with targeted communication to request they participate as sponsors.

Creating a network of support with sponsors, managers and key influencers builds an informal network to assess and determine the overall feeling about the change, and gaps in readiness and support. For larger change programs, structured governance committees can highlight what's happening across the organization. This provides an opportunity for two-way communication to activate the change conversation across multiple groups.

Sponsors and Key Stakeholders Identified

TRACKING MINDSET CHANGE WITH PERSONAS AND JOURNEY MAPS

At the heart of all successful change is personal, individual change. Leaders tend to manage change at the team or organization level. They might add a new project management tool, believing it will make the creative team more efficient. But successful change only happens when *individuals* willingly adopt the new tool, and some element of their working life improves because of it. As the adage goes, "Change is a door that can only be opened from the inside."

People don't experience change in the same way or at the same time. Some team members may understand impacts and are ready to get going right away, while others may look for ways to delay changes to their work to maintain the status quo for as long as possible.

To encourage forward movement through a change, you need to understand how individual needs evolve along the way and meet people where they are in their change journey, offer support during the transition, and stay connected during the change process. Personas and Journey Maps help you do this. *(Download the Persona and Journey Map templates at* changefatigue.com.*)*

Personas and Journey Maps are common tools in marketing, service design, user research, and product development to help track the mindset change a customer must experience as they consider, purchase, use, and repurchase a product or service. In our change facilitation work, we've adapted customer-focused Personas and Journey Maps to internal change initiatives to identify when different levels of effort will be needed to support communications, training, and engagement for the change initiative.

Personas. Depending on the scale of the change, your list of impacted individuals from the Stakeholder Assessment Matrix could be quite long. It can be overwhelming to consider how to engage each of those individuals, and leaders often default to thinking about how change will impact various teams or departments.

A more useful way to group and simplify early thinking about who is impacted is to use Personas to group together people who will likely need similar messaging and engagement.

Personas are groups of people who are likely to behave in similar ways in a given situation.

In the example of a company adopting a new Intranet, high power impacted managers who are skeptical or resistant might be grouped into a "Priority Win" Persona that gets priority attention early in the change process to win them over to the Promoter mindset. Apathetic staff and users might get grouped into a "Need to Know" Persona that gets infrequent updates just to keep them in the loop.

Once you identify Personas, you'll notice that throughout the change journey, various Personas may need very little communication while others will require dedicating serious time to the change.

For example, one of your Personas is "sponsors," which we discussed earlier in this chapter. Now is the time to reach out to that Persona group to request their sponsorship.

Later in the change process each and every impacted individual may need to be identified for things like training needs and user permissions for I.T. We use Journey Maps to determine what Personas need along the change timeline.

Journey Maps. Personas help identify *who* will be impacted and Journey Maps reveal *when* various staff will need extra support to move to the next stage and *when* they might need to dedicate actual work hours to the change implementation. This helps managers schedule time to support the change and helps change leaders know when and how to communicate.

In the initial stages of awareness about the change, engagement efforts may showcase the reasons for the change, but as the initiative matures, the volume of communication targeted at specific Personas (and eventually specific people) will also change. You can use Journey Maps to plan for this.

To provide the right support, leaders need to understand what obstacles may be preventing the change from happening right now. For smaller, incremental change, it may be a problem around awareness; people simply don't know about a new way of working. For transformative or larger scale change, it may be due to the lack of specialized skills to implement and manage the change. **Questions to ask when building a Journey Map:**

— Will some Personas have to change more or less than others (workload, processes, team structure)?

— Which Personas need to be informed more frequently or more in depth based on your assessment?

— How will training be customized by Persona?

— What support will be provided to individuals, teams, and managers?

— When will phases of the change come into effect for different teams or individuals?

How This Works in the Real World

We worked with a team who was building a new project management tool for tracking major research reports. Phase One of that change involved defining the decision framework, writing a requirements document and the RFP, and selecting a tool to pilot with a group of senior report authors *(Senior Author Persona)* who were very familiar with the process. There were also discussions with technical staff *(I.T. Persona)*, and the procurement team *(Executive Persona)* got involved in the details as well.

We pulled in a different group of report writers, designers, and communications staff who would use the tool (*Tool Users Persona*) to test and populate the tool, as well as write the first draft of procedures. This group helped define the specifics, and also later served as change champions, building support on their teams so everyone is on board.

One team really wanted the ability to link to the final files online and in the internal file-sharing system, but the extra convenience was deemed not worth the expense. This is the phase where the first resistance showed up. We heard people grumbling about the effort required to change the process. — *"This will never work."*

— *"We have never been successful in these kinds of things in the past ... remember what happened last time?"*

— *"What! Another change to manage? This is the third request this month."*

To overcome these initial reactions, we had to develop messaging customized to the Tool Users Persona to clarify what was changing and what was not, the reasoning behind the change, and what would remain unchanged. We worked to ignite their imaginations about what was possible and set reasonable expectations about what this particular change initiative would achieve.

As the project moved into implementation and adoption, the change leader developed incentives for the Tool Users to update their work daily, highlighting active users in staff meetings and using the tool as input for important promotion efforts. Reports to track adoption were built to help managers know who needed additional training or encouragement.

Some Personas were more involved than others at each step along the way. But, by the end, everyone felt they had had the opportunity to enhance the tool as it was being developed and they understood why various decisions were made, even if they didn't agree with them.

By understanding where team members are in their personal change journey, you can adjust messaging, tackle resistance, assess readiness and develop a training plan that actually works because it meets them where they are.

MAP THE CHANGE JOURNEY

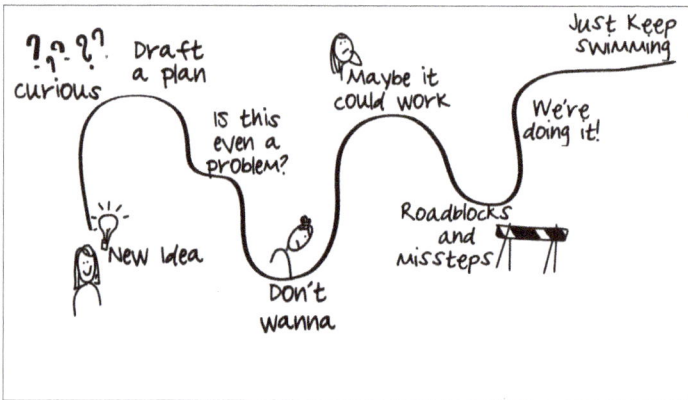

Visit changefatigue.com *for the Journey Map template and other resources*

The Stakeholder Assessment Matrix, along with Personas and Journey Map work helps you identify individuals or groups of individuals who need active, priority communication to gain their support for the change initiative. The best way to gauge their readiness and understand their perspective is to ask them. This is the role for a change facilitator and confidential inquiry.

CONFIDENTIAL INQUIRY

No project starts with a blank slate. The context around the initiative is the soil where you're planting the change seed— and the weather in the forecast. No decent gardener would plant a delicate shrub among rocks in winter.

Prepare the team for the change by understanding the origin of the project, identifying constraints, evaluating past efforts to solve similar problems, and bringing team politics out in the open. This will help identify risks to your success and avoid issues that could threaten the outcome. It's also valuable to understand the concerns individuals on the team have about the change. Understanding your stakeholder's perspective on all these things is crucial. But how do you get them to 'fess up and tell you what they really think? Enter Confidential Inquiry.

Confidential Inquiry is a specific style of stakeholder interview designed to put the individual at ease and gain true insights about the proposed change from their perspective. These insights are ideally rolled up into broad themes or findings and reported back to the change initiative leaders to refine either the change itself, (e.g., the feedback is the change is happening way too fast, we need to slow down the milestones) or how the change is being communicated. (E.g., the feedback is that the communication is full of jargon, and no one really understands how their role will be impacted.)

Identify the change facilitator. This is one area where it really helps to have a dedicated external change facilitator gathering these insights confidentially. This isn't just about hopping on the phone for 15 minutes to gather feedback. Calls like that don't get at the heart of the change, and the feedback focuses on typos in the document or nitpicky comments around the margins of the change. The stakeholder being interviewed needs to feel confident that the insights they share will not come back to bite them later, or else they won't share their real concerns. Nothing they say in the session should in any way be repeated or hinted at in a way that could identify them. When the change facilitator is introduced to the project, they should be positioned as a neutral party, not an extension of the executive team, gathering insights and concerns and advocating for them with whoever has authority to fix any negative issues they are willing to share.

The change facilitator reiterates the commitment to anonymity and how all comments will be anonymized before any type of sharing. They don't record interviews or share notes directly from the interviews. The goal of these conversations is learning from the team, and it is the job of the change facilitator to summarize feedback into broad themes in a way that provides anonymity.

Because these interviews take time, some teams try to skip this step, believing that they understand all they need to, and no essential insights will emerge from this type of work. In our experience, that is not the case. Confidential Inquiry routinely uncovers significant unidentified resistance and blockers to the initiative that could derail or significantly delay the project. The time invested to learn almost always pays huge dividends.

One of the strongest arguments for outsourcing these conversations to a trained change facilitator is that a significant part of the process is building rapport. At this point in the process, the stakeholder has very little to gain and a lot to lose by sharing valid, valuable concerns. If they are assured anonymity, they often view an external interviewer as more objective. In addition, a trained change facilitator has expertise in quickly gathering the most relevant insights. One strategy that we and other trained change facilitators use is the FBI's Behavioral Change Stairway Model.

A trained change facilitator begins the Confidential Inquiry session by describing the issue from the point of view of those impacted, describing the proposed change, and outlining how that solution is supposed to benefit others and at what cost (time, resources, taking attention from other priorities). From here the interview usually enters a conversational stage, with the change facilitator often using the five-step crisis communications process known as the Behavioral Change Stairway Model (BCSM).[13] The format is incredibly helpful as a model for Confidential Inquiry, addressing the important rapport-building first steps that come ahead of gathering deep insights or influencing opinions about the topic of the interview.

In this context, the "behavioral change" we're working towards is open-minded conversation and evaluation of a new way of working that the interviewee may be skeptical or even hostile to considering. As a leader considering whether to invest the time and energy in this phase, it is useful to consider the basics of the Behavioral Change Stairway Model.

Active Listening. Former head of FBI international hostage negotiation, Chris Voss said, "Your first objective in the negotiation, instead of making your argument, is to hear the other side out."[14]

It's crucial for the interviewer not to disagree or even evaluate anything the stakeholder says at this point. Even if their skepticism is unfounded or their statements are provably false, the stakeholder is trying to share how it *feels* from where they sit, and that is valuable information. The interviewer validates however they are feeling right now.

Empathy. Empathy is the ability to truly, deeply understand what is going on for this person and what is motivating them to act or share as they do. Empathy is really the secret weapon because it uncovers what motivates and deters us from change.

Most of the time stakeholders are invited to these stakeholder interviews during the "messy middle" of the change. Some planning has occurred, there is some speculation about how the organization will move forward, but nothing is decided and the path ahead is unclear.

A good metaphor for this moment is a snow globe that has just been shaken up. In this stage of the process the team members can't see (empathize with) each other or have a clear vision of what's ahead. When the change facilitator empathizes with the stakeholder, it allows feelings to settle and invites their rational mind to a conversation about pros and cons of the current versus future state.

Rapport. If empathy is when the stakeholder feels the facilitator understands their perspective, rapport is the stage that happens when they feel the change facilitator agrees. Until this stage, the conversation has been mostly one sided, with the facilitator mostly silent and actively listening. Rapport is defined as building a relationship of mutual trust and affinity, and as rapport is achieved the conversation turns into a more robust dialog, with facilitator and stakeholder collaborating on new ways of defining the problem or ways the proposed solution (or a different one) could be most effective in solving the problem.

Influence. The next phase of the conversation should be about aligning on a shared vision of success.

The goal is to help them imagine a world where this issue disappears. What would it take to resolve this challenge? It can be useful to encourage them to dream big and set aside known constraints in order to find new pathways, stepping stones to get to a new reality. The facilitator returns at this point to the details of the problem and proposed solution, in order to build a shared understanding of the organizational roadmap.

From a change perspective, these interviews give stakeholders a safe place to "think out loud." This effort helps them build new ideas and language that they often feel empowered to share directly in future planning sessions with the leaders of the change initiative.

Behavior Change. The final step of the stairway model is Behavior Change. In Confidential Inquiry, the facilitator is trying to coach the stakeholder to change their perspective on the proposed change and open their minds to the possibility of success. A secondary goal is to encourage them to become a sponsor or advocate for the change in their spheres of influence.

As the leader and change facilitator work to plan these Confidential Inquiry interviewers, this interview guide should help align on the materials and perspective the change facilitator will share as they guide the stakeholder through the interview.

Build the confidential inquiry guide. As you work with a change facilitator to decide how to approach Confidential Inquiry, consider our list of questions available in the Confidential Inquiry Guide at changefatigue.com.

Bottom line: the role of the change facilitator is to get at very personal perspectives that may be perceived as critical or even unsupportive if delivered directly to the change leaders. **Giving relevant stakeholders a chance to voice those concerns in a safe space is a critical path to building trust.**

The change facilitator is also well positioned during the interview to correct any misconceptions about the proposed change, fill in any gaps in understanding between the change leaders and the stakeholder, and offer to take their main concerns back to leaders in a way that won't be attributed to them or cause them any negative outcomes. All of this is incredibly important for winning over stakeholders whose support and engagement is essential to the success of the project.

▸ MILESTONE ACHIEVED

Stakeholder Perspectives Documented

MOVING FROM COMMUNICATION TO ENGAGEMENT

The next step in selling the change involves communicating with impacted groups of stakeholders and trying to increase their engagement with the change. This may include engagement activities like presenting information about the change as part of their regularly scheduled team meetings, "Ask Me Anything" (AMA) sessions, town halls with surveys before and after, or a *change roadshow* (bringing small groups of stakeholders together to review the Change Summary to get feedback and buy-in). Share information on the channels where people will access it. Tap into existing networks and meetings to share messaging.

Here are the most vital topics you should cover when communicating the change in smaller groups.

Key elements of an engagement script:

— What isn't working in the current state

— What issues this change will resolve

— Who has been consulted on the scope of the problem and proposed solution to date

— How the change will benefit the people in this meeting

— What isn't changing

— Opportunities for people in this meeting to grow or change roles

— What criteria was used to determine who would be moving into new roles

— Specifics about how the change can realistically improve their day-to-day work

— Timing and scope of the work

— How individuals in the meeting can impact the roadmap and progress of the proposed change

---

Allow people to ask questions in the session. Their questions will help you gain an understanding of where they may be in the change cycle. Address all questions, even if you run out of time; let them know where they can go to access the answers after the meeting. In addition, simply listening to someone who feels powerless can create a big boost in their level of trust in whatever decision is on the table. For contentious issues, remind the team about a respectful workplace and that their questions are an opportunity to clarify not condone the change. Welcome feedback but discourage complaining.

It's also critical to be realistic. Don't sell false promises or make the new workload seem lighter than it will be. People can gear up for anything but if you've sold them sunshine and unicorns, they're going to be unhappy even with a nice walk in the park.

Use communication best practices. A communications plan is simply a map of who needs to know what information, and when they need to know it. The Stakeholder Assessment is a useful starting point for defining Personas who will need the same types of communications on the same timeline. Depending on the communication platforms your team uses, this may mean setting up email lists or communication groups (e.g., Slack channel or Microsoft Teams) based on impacted Personas.

Depending on the scope and complexity of the change initiative, your communications plan might fit on a single page or consist of multiple messaging campaigns. The point is to consider ways to develop, deliver, and manage communications efforts in order to gather feedback, address concerns, and reduce resistance.

Ensure that you don't just share for the sake of transparency, but instead have a specific purpose in what you share when.

How This Works in the Real World

We worked with an organization where the senior leadership spent a year in planning sessions coordinating a strategic vision but had not yet made some critical decisions. *Would the changes require a reorganization? Would some teams lose headcount or resources?*

Because these leaders had spent so long with big ideas and along the way had interviewed and engaged some stakeholders who talked with other staff, they decided it was time to update the entire organization.

However, because so many of the questions affecting staff were still unanswered, workers across departments felt widespread concern about how the strategic changes would impact their roles. These were questions that leaders were not yet ready to answer. So, they spent considerable effort after that company-wide meeting tamping down concern and rebuilding trust in the planning process.

Our "In the Real World" example shows why Persona and Journey Map work comes in very handy as leaders determine what they should share and the appropriate timeline for sharing with key groups of stakeholders. To begin outlining the known, high-level communications that will be needed, create a new Communications Plan tab in your Stakeholder Assessment Matrix with the following columns:

— Audience (Persona)

— Related milestone

— Key Message

— Channel

— Messenger

— Approvals needed

Follow guidelines for effective change communication. *(Find the Communications Plan in the Stakeholder Assessment Matrix template at changefatigue.com.)*

Target messages to specific audiences and milestones. Messaging too early, too often, or in the wrong channels can lead to your audience tuning out. Initial communications may cast a wide invitation to broadly describe the problem and offer opportunities to weigh in, but after the change initiative begins, communications should be mapped to project milestones and highly targeted to specific Personas.

Repeat, repeat, repeat. Once you know your messages are intentional and targeted, don't be afraid to repeat yourself. You can append updates and "FYI" communications to existing newsletters, staff communications, and team meetings in addition to sending standalone messages to specific Personas.

"When you're tired of your message, it's just starting to land."

—Adam Grant

Be clear about requests and accountability. Each communication should have a clear call to action. The reader should know exactly what they need to do next. Specifically, call out that "no response" will be interpreted as tacit approval to continue. Set expectations for when future milestones will be available for review and comment.

Welcome all feedback. Ensure opportunities for feedback are easy and have no negative repercussions. Consider providing feedback options that are anonymous or via a neutral third party. Address questions and ask for feedback at town halls, roadshow presentations, small group meetings, or at any open discussion meeting. Track questions and answers to help drive key messaging and website content.

Choose the right messenger. Employees prefer to hear organizational messages from executives and senior leaders, and personal messages from their supervisors and managers.[15]

Be realistic. Not everything will work in the pilot phase. Bugs will come up and new processes will need to evolve.

MORE OF	LESS OF
Clear, targeted and tailored communications	Generic messages blasted to everyone
Proactive and structured communications	Last-minute and reactive
Supporting managers as messangers	Expecting managers to translate to their team
Communicating on their preferred channels	Communicating mainly by email or "the grapevine"

When you acknowledge the difficulties and help your staff understand that the implementation dip is an expected part of the process (more on that in Chapter Four), those affected will more likely put negative responses in context and see the light at the end of the tunnel. Try to keep the "messy middle" away from stakeholders who are not directly affected until major questions are answered or most of the kinks are worked out.

▸ MILESTONE ACHIEVED

Communications Roadmap Outlined

Chapters One and Two take up more than a third of this book because in our work, we've found it's not just important to lay a firm foundation—it's impossible to create lasting change without one.

You've defined the problem as a group and identified a solution that addresses as many stakeholder concerns as possible. You have sponsor support and a communication plan and you're rolling out the message to key groups.

You're as prepared as you can be, but know that all the preparation in the world won't prevent at least a little resistance. In Chapter Three we'll discuss how to deal with the inevitable (and very normal) resistance and power struggles.

03

ADDRESS RESISTANCE AND POWER STRUGGLES

A plan can have sound strategy, backed by data, but that doesn't mean the team is buying it.

An idea that makes perfect sense on paper can still be rejected in practice. Key considerations like whose job gets easier or harder, who gets credit or extra resources, individual aversion to risk, and change fatigue all affect buy-in for a new plan.

To tackle the resistance that comes from these sources, change leaders need to prepare for roadblocks and work to dismantle them in advance. This starts with addressing the attitudes and beliefs of everyone affected by the change.

From new ways of working (including performance standards), and new ways of thinking (Hello, growth mindset!) leaders have an important role to play. Setting expectations and taking a different perspective supports both top-down and bottom-up thinking. It requires a better understanding and respect of lived experiences of the people that have different skills and knowledge than the leadership team enacting the change.

CHANGE READINESS REDUCES RESISTANCE

Change leaders can help address resistance not only through actively coaching teams, but through leading by example. New processes and new ideas will challenge old beliefs and thinking, and every time they do, there's an opportunity to model how to handle that challenge.

> ## "Accept the obstacle and work with what you're given."
> —Marcus Aurelius

Resistance is a natural reaction to uncertainty, so it's important to see the change from their perspective so that you can clarify their gains and clear up any misconceptions. Success or failure in previous changes, the current amount of change fatigue, consequences of the change and how stakeholders have been introduced and involved with past change efforts have a big impact on levels of resistance.

These factors are typically "out of your hands" so the readiness can be a better place to focus attention. The earlier work in Chapters One and Two helped identify the people you need to involve and fears they may have. Now is when you will use that knowledge to anticipate resistance so that you can reduce or remove it.

How to know if you're encountering resistance. In some teams, resistance and objections are obvious, while in others, the "back channels" drive undercover resistance. This hidden resistance can seriously hinder progress because it's not shared publicly and therefore is much less likely to be addressed early.

Change leaders need to support both the macro (organizational) perspective and micro (individual) perspective. In Chapter Five, we share details for how to evaluate and adjust team culture and individual support for new ways of working. To foster change readiness among stakeholders, a change leader must work to sway the attitudes, plans, and behavior of people involved in the change.

Team members will look to one another to understand the significance of the change they are facing. That means change leaders need to address the beliefs, attitudes, intentions and behavior of change participants, who then go on to influence each other's views of the change. This view accentuates the social aspects of change as organizational players look to one another for clues about the meaning of events and circumstances facing the organization.[16]

Set up a management huddle. One way to address competing requirements of change is to set up a leadership coaching huddle for managers. During the huddle:

— share the current state of change.
— ask managers about current stresses for each team.

— ask about how team members are managing workloads and where work-life balance might already be suffering.

This kind of management huddle allows influential managers to ask questions about the change. It also allows leaders to address and reduce stress from different sources in advance of the change initiative, and ensure transparency among managers, whose support will be vital.

Once you have gathered a list of stressors from your managers, compare them to this list, identified by recent industry benchmarking[17] as the top reasons people resist change:

— Unclear or don't agree with the reason for the change (*"What's in it for me?"*)

— Required changes in job roles (like increasing workload, new behavioral requirements or lack of time)

— Fear from uncertainty or prior experience with failed change

— Lack of support from and trust in management or leadership including poor role modeling

— Lack of inclusion in the change contributed to frustration about upcoming changes

Do you see parallels between this list and the information you gathered in the huddles? Use this list as an agenda for continued conversations with stakeholders and think about ways to remove resistance through more communication, time, or help available.

LOCATING THE SOURCE OF RESISTANCE: SUBCONSCIOUS VS. RATIONAL CONCERNS

Decades of neuroscience research have demonstrated that our emotions, sometimes even subconscious ones, dramatically influence our judgments and choices.[18] Scientists talk about two main regions of the brain influencing decision making: the prefrontal cortex or the "rational brain" and the brain stem or "lizard brain," which is the most primitive part of the brain, operating based on instinct rather than thoughtful, conscious evaluation.

Change leaders need to understand that for many people, even the mention of change activates a deep, sometimes subconscious, fear in the lizard brain, making it difficult for the facts of the change to make it to the prefrontal cortex for rational evaluation. People respond defensively and resist.

Their emotional mind (a.k.a. lizard brain) is afraid the change will cost them power or autonomy and they prefer things how they are, thank you very much.

Because of how we're wired as humans, the emotional mind has to feel in control of its own destiny before the rational mind can evaluate anything based on facts and logic. That's why we recommend you begin addressing resistance by identifying and addressing "lizard brain" fears.

Calm the lizard brain fears. Most change initiatives bring with them a change in responsibilities that results in a power shift across a team or even an entire organization. Stakeholders know this, which is why when changes are on the horizon, the first response is often defensive. The question everyone wants to be answered is, "what negative effects might this have on me and my job?"

— Will I still have a job after the change?

— Will I have to learn new skills?

— Will others get new resources and how do I get my share of those?

— Will extra responsibilities be distributed and rewarded fairly?
...and dozens more

Without trust and buy-in, leaders can expect to see roadblock after roadblock get thrown up as those not on board dig in their heels, "wait and see" or grab for power.

To calm fears and address concerns, leaders should have clear answers ready, preferably before anyone even asks the question. See Chapter One on solving the right problem and aligning incentives. Resistance can also signal that you don't have alignment on the actual problem or the solution criteria. Go back to agreement on the root cause and the problem statement.

Depending on the initiative, it can also be useful to acknowledge the "messy middle" and how the team will deal with bumps in the road along the way. Organizations with a culture of experimentation and a healthy relationship to learning from failure will have an easier time venturing into this stage. Leaders can cultivate these skills in advance to help build a healthy team ready for change. We'll talk about healthy team norms and psychological safety in Chapter Five.

Turn rational resistance into feedback. Once you've calmed some underlying fears, it becomes easier to address resistance about whether the change will actually work.

When stakeholders evaluate the details of the change, they may have perfectly rational skepticism. Listen for questions like, "Will this plan meet our objectives?" or "How will this help me do X?"

If those impacted by the change can't confidently get on board, at best, they'll drag their feet on participating, and at worst they become loud detractors. Whenever possible, look for procrastinators and resisters and single them out for Confidential Inquiry and feedback *before* their resistance cements.

Leaders are more likely to gain valuable insights from people who disagree than from initiative advocates and allies. Resisters should be sought out and respected for two reasons. First, they sometimes have ideas missing from the decision framework, especially in situations with a lot of diversity or complexity. Second, resisters are crucial when it comes to the politics of implementation. Sharing power with them often disarms the fight and wins them over, improving their confidence and support for the project.

Follow **our Persuasion Checklist for disarming resistance.** When a resister voices concerns when a plan is already headed to implementation, pull out the Persuasion Checklist:

☐ Were they part of the decision framework and solution brainstorming? If not, walk them through who participated and how the decision to implement this idea was agreed upon. **Key takeaway: This was a team decision.**

☐ Do they have an emotional fear they're not comfortable sharing? Consider a Confidential Inquiry session to create a safe place for that feedback.

Key takeaway: We're trying to make this fair, safe, and equitable across the team.

☐ Do they have rational concerns that the leadership team needs to hear? Gather their feedback, check with their peers to see if others have similar concerns, and report back to them about whether that issue will be mitigated.
Key takeaway: We're always learning, and welcome feedback at every stage.

Note: not everyone can be persuaded. Some team members will be too committed to their opposition, but most of the time this approach defuses the most adamant resistance that blocks the change from happening, often transforming loud objections into reluctant acceptance which, while not ideal, is definitely an improvement.

These persuasion efforts are really about increasing trust between the resister and the decision-makers. As Stephen M. R. Covey said, "Innovation happens at the speed of trust."[19] Distrust halts action toward change and innovation.

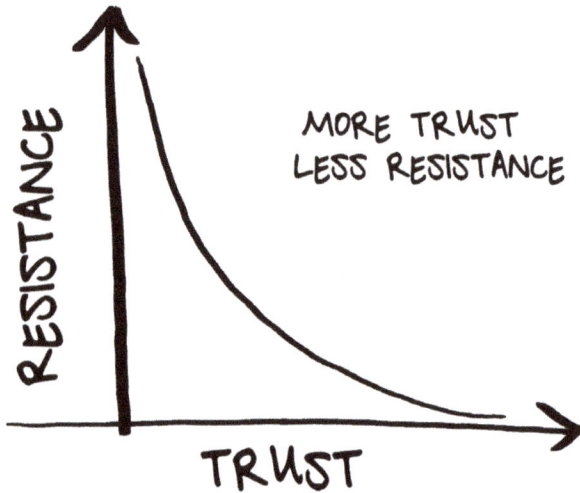

RESISTANCE

MORE TRUST
LESS RESISTANCE

TRUST

DISARM POWER STRUGGLES WITH POWER SHARING

Power struggles come from trying to change the behavior of another person without their agreement. A leader may have enough power to force a decision or behavior in the moment, but they can't force anyone on the team to change their mind. Almost every power struggle comes from a series of missed opportunities to build alignment in small ways.

Big problems are usually tiny problems that were ignored.

LITTLE PROBLEM

BIG PROBLEM!

Over time

By the time everyone is committed to their own favorite version of, for instance, a new company logo, it's going to be a lot harder to win trust and get to agreement.

Leaders can, however, create an environment where the team is more likely to *want* to do what they suggest. If you are a leader in charge of doling out projects and praise, authority and autonomy, you already have everything you need to align a team. And even if you're not the designated leader of the team, you still have some power. Every one of us confers power when attention, support, and resources are shared with others.

Micro-negotiate. Most leaders think about negotiating as something they do in the hiring process, but really every day holds opportunities to decide how to allocate the resources of time, attention, praise, power, autonomy and more. Every single tiny interaction is an opportunity for a tiny amount of power to change hands; in our work we refer to this as a "micro-negotiation."

Micro-negotiations build trust, and they allow people to feel powerful. When people feel powerful along the way, they are less likely to resist and more likely to assess the proposed change rationally.

If you work to share power around the less significant things *(Where is the meeting being held? Who will speak first?)* you'll earn trust and buy-in. By the time you're selecting a vendor or finalizing the budget, team members are able to trust that their opinions are valued instead of digging in for a power struggle.

"*All leadership is influence.*"

—Dr. John C. Maxwell

TIPS FOR POWER SHARING:

1. **Drop the ego.** Successful leaders know it doesn't matter who does the work, how they choose to do it, or who gets credit, as long as it gets done. Does the overall plan get better or worse if you let others have some power and control?

2. **Know what you're willing to give up.** If you're asking your team to work harder in one area, it can be useful to have a few ideas about areas where they can slow down or take pressure off. Know what you're willing to trade. It's also helpful to ask for a little more than you actually need, (e.g., you ask for the team to produce a new report weekly, but you know that every other week would likely be fine), so that if you can't get exactly what you asked for, you can at least get a version that meets the basic goals.

3. **"Lose" on purpose.** Trying to get your way on every decision will cause a power struggle that costs you the big picture. Especially with the smaller decisions, cede the floor with grace and let your team feel powerful and in control. If tensions are high, and you advocate for a particular solution but then agree to a route suggested by one of your team members, this can go a long way toward building trust.

► MILESTONE ACHIEVED

Resistance Identified and Disarmed

In these ways, you can build a work environment where your teams are not only happier but are also more willing to support and promote upcoming changes.

Resistance is best addressed by beginning in-person conversations early; listening even when the feedback is not what you want to hear; and truthfully answering questions, even if the answer is "we don't know yet, but I will let you know when we do."

Be confident in the aspects of your plan that you have nailed down, even if you haven't determined every aspect. See those unknowns as an asset: they allow you to adjust communication as more information becomes available.

Finally, consider that all communication has both verbal and nonverbal aspects. Tone of voice, words, and body language convey a big part of the story. According to the Albert Mehrabian "7-38-55 Rule," spoken word only conveys 7 percent of meaning, vocal tonality accounts for 38 percent, and body language accounts for 55 percent.[20] Watch for reactions as you share information to identify and address resistance.

04

BALANCE MOTIVATIONS AND WORKLOADS

Now that you have addressed resistance and power struggles, you as the change leader can turn attention to helping teams respond to the new tasks the change initiative will bring and how workloads might need to be adjusted for new tasks and processes.

Successful team leaders match tasks and even change how solutions are designed and implemented to better align with individual skills and motivations. Luckily, this is not a talent that leaders are born with—it's a skill that can be learned.

Getting creative with the workload requires a few prerequisites:

— Everyone has to understand required tasks and priorities.

— Individuals must be honest about what they're good at and what they really can't stand doing, and leaders need to encourage this honesty because they see it increases the team's overall efficiency: when leaders understand everyone's skill set, they put the players in the right positions on the field, so to speak.

— The assignment of tasks needs to serve two masters—the capabilities and motivations of the individuals and the organization's need to achieve goals efficiently.

This planning ensures individuals who are asked to make the change know what is expected of them and have support, even when the work gets especially hard or stressful.

FLEX THE SOLUTION TO MATCH TEAM MEMBERS' MOTIVATIONS

Below, we will discuss three ways to flex the solution to match motivations: identifying individual motivations, allocating tasks by capabilities, and uncovering hidden work.

Identify individual motivations. So, how do team leaders ensure tasks and individuals are properly matched? One component of a match is their capabilities (what they can do), and the other is their motivation (what they want to do). We'll talk about capabilities in the next section. Let's start by addressing how team leaders can identify individual motivations.

Motivation can be broken down into three major elements.

1. **Behavior:** the skills, processes, and tools individuals prefer to use as they deliver their work

2. **Mindset:** how individuals relate their work back to their identity and their larger purpose in life

3. **Incentives:** how individuals prefer to be rewarded

These are the levers team leaders can adjust to maximize job satisfaction and sustainable change adoption.

People don't all enjoy the same rewards or want the same power and control. Running a meeting is invigorating for some people and absolutely terrifying for others. Some people feel empowered when they are praised in front of their teammates, while others prefer behind-the-scenes encouragement from a leader they respect.

One science-backed model to help with engagement is the SCARF Model, which identifies five areas of motivation: **S**tatus, **C**ertainty, **A**utonomy, **R**elatedness, and **F**airness.[21] This model can help identify and minimize the threats perceived by the lizard brain and maximize rewards based on individual needs.

A new change initiative is an excellent opportunity to review and refresh the roles people play and the specific tasks within those roles they find rewarding. Here are some specific examples to consider.

BEHAVIOR

— **Autonomy:** Do they want the freedom to direct their own work or prefer to check things off a defined list of assigned work?

— **Mastery:** Do they seek opportunities to learn and demonstrate new skills?

MINDSET

— **Leadership:** Do they prefer to take control of projects or situations, or do they function better as an individual contributor?

— **Growth and Development:** Do they have bigger ambitions for their career trajectory? Do they have a side project or personal hobby related to their work?

INCENTIVES

— **Recognition:** Do they prefer private or public recognition? Whose appreciation would they most value?

— **Compensation:** Are they more likely to be motivated by financial incentives, flexibility, or some other benefit?

Everyone wants something: happiness is in the right match.

How This Works in the Real World

We worked with a cross-functional team that was brought together to support the introduction of a new technology platform. The working group was made up of team members from different parts of the business which historically had competed for the same budget to deliver work. In addition, they had little or no exposure to each other. The change leader noticed a reluctance to "mix the waters" across teams.

During the kick-off sessions, the leader introduced the importance of working together. The larger group was split into smaller groups where each team member shared a series of questions to uncover preferences around communication, ways of working, motivations and feedback. Then, this information was summarized and brought back to the broader group to create transparency and build trust. By addressing the reluctance head on, the team was able to shift the focus to considering the wants and needs of others.

But how do team leaders know what individuals want and what motivates them? As you saw in our "In the Real World" example, team leaders must listen and observe first.

Watch for what lights them up. Ask explicitly about what work comes easily and feels rewarding.

By listening, you as the change leader are investing in relationships and creating an environment in which the team feels comfortable. Relationships drive collaborative projects, regardless of the size of the change. When you spend the time to understand team members as individuals, you are making it easier for the team to stay intact and strong throughout the change process, and you're making it more likely that change will stick.

> "If we want to say something in a way that others will hear, we have to think about them, about their values and their frames of reference—not just about ourselves."
>
> —Margaret Heffernen

Allocate tasks by capabilities. Most everyday tasks are assigned based not on who would be the best person to complete the work but on job descriptions and where individuals sit on the team.

This way of allocating work makes sense in traditional work environments: the worker with the riveting gun at their station will insert all the rivets. But in knowledge work, where teams are working together to solve complex problems, the talents of individuals don't always neatly align with where they sit in the organizational chart.

This means that the complex job of organizing information across multiple data sources or analyzing performance metrics may be assigned to the person who needs the answers, not the person who is exceptional at Excel functions or data analysis.

Asking people to do work they are not naturally good at is demoralizing and frustrating to the individual and inefficient for the team's performance.

Today's traditional hierarchical org chart often doesn't flex to changing conditions. In real life, team members often juggle multiple tasks that can be hard to narrow into a succinct job title or role description. Depending on the context, different roles can step into leading or supporting positions or can be accountable for some of the work, but only informed about other work.

Meaningful work is equal parts curiosity, impact, and mastery.

The important thing is to create a clear picture of how each role supports the whole team and the specific change initiative, even as things evolve. Visibility around how everyone makes and keeps commitments is critical.

YOUR JOB AS CHANGE LEADER IS TO ADVOCATE FOR A WORK ENVIRONMENT WHERE:

— everyone knows the activities required to meet defined performance metrics and what is necessary to meet career development goals.

— leadership has the necessary conversations to define new job requirements as a result of the change and discuss potential matching.

— roles are clearly defined, including key outcomes of the role; relationship to other roles; and how the team will come together to support organizational goals and objectives.

The best teams save energy for what really matters and ignore the rest. Aligning tasks with capabilities helps the team do that. Start by identifying tasks that drain energy, and consider opportunities to remove from the task list altogether; to deprioritize the work so it consumes less energy; or find out if someone else doesn't mind this task and swap or outsource.

Uncover and account for hidden work. In all of the teams we've worked with over the past twenty years, team members take on invisible work to get tasks done. Tanya Reid calls this "glue work" which is less glamorous (and often less promotable) work that needs to happen to make a team successful.[22]

If you've ever had someone come up and ask for a small thing like reviewing a document or talking through a challenge, you know firsthand the impact of the "side of the desk" request. The adage, "If you want something done, ask a busy person to do it," is often adopted by team members trying to balance their own workloads. It may not seem like a lot to ask a quick favor, but those small requests add up. Often, people who don't have the capacity to do the task find it hard to say no.

Many teams don't account for the time people invest in these small favors. Consider creating a team log of "side of the desk" activities. Have frank conversations about work assignments. Your Journey Map can help you dig deeper into the experience of team members. Encourage team members to think before they ask and ensure this work is accounted for in the larger plan. This will help define the actual workload and areas where your team members may struggle to adopt the change.

Also use your Journey Map to identify when work will ramp up. Communicate beforehand to help your team prepare for the added pressure, and ask questions about how things are going and how people are feeling about the upcoming change. Connect with and visit staff on the front line of the change to understand their needs and remove any obstacles in their way.

To ensure that hidden work doesn't derail projects, team leaders should understand how the team gets work done, and should be able to communicate that to change leaders as much as possible, since this information is vital to balancing the workload.

And as the change leader, be sure you know what motivates YOU to maintain the enthusiasm. Change management is often invisible work, but it is critical for the success of any project.

How This Works in the Real World

We worked with a leader who had done some initial change work and was excited to announce the benefits the change would bring. She organized a meeting with her leadership team to share the scope of the change. But she had not considered how the leadership team would react to the update in light of two other initiatives that had also recently been approved. At the end of the meeting, she opened up the session for questions. Someone asked, "How do you plan to duplicate our team to make this scalable? We're already working overtime to meet the current schedule, and what you're proposing is simply impossible."

Several other members chimed in. The energy around the initiative shifted from an exciting opportunity to dread. More work!

She learned that understanding dependencies and the current workload is the first step in assigning tasks as part of a change initiative. Through a roadmap session, team members gathered to look at all work in progress. Then, through a priority discussion, work was scheduled for later delivery, and new staff from other teams were brought in during the transition.

▸ MILESTONE ACHIEVED

Workloads Balanced to Support Adoption

TAKEAWAYS FOR BALANCING WORKLOAD TO MATCH MOTIVATIONS

Prepare yourself and your team for the ups and downs in workload that come with change implementation. When you acknowledge the difficulties, those affected will be more likely to put any negative responses in context and see the light at the end of the tunnel. As you and the team make your way through change implementation, revisit power dynamics at milestone moments and consider ways to distribute new tasks and authority equitably.

When team members in charge of implementing the change know that their work is valued and that workloads will be adjusted based on what is negotiable and non-negotiable, they adjust and reset their expectations. As you'll see in Chapter Five, this helps create a sense of team safety that is vital to supporting successful, sustained change.

05

HEALTHY TEAM NORMS AND PSYCHOLOGICAL SAFETY

Let's say you follow all the advice in this book. You get input in identifying the problem and in choosing the solution. You sell the vision, turn resistance into feedback, devise ways to share power, and balance workloads.

You're golden, right? Maybe.

Here's the thing: you can do all those things in good faith and still have trouble getting the change to stick if you have not addressed team norms. Most teams fail at change because they fail at teamwork.

If you don't have healthy team norms, you probably struggled through all the steps in Chapters One through Four. Still, if you were tenacious, you might have made it through. But for the change to become lasting and therefore beneficial, you must address team norms and psychological safety.

As mentioned at the top of the book, high-functioning teams are much more likely to be nimble and open to change. You may assume your team is "high functioning." But how do you know?

Or maybe you know your team tends to be more rigid and slow moving, but you have no idea what to do about it.

We'll share some concrete ideas here, as well as share what the research has shown: high-functioning teams are defined by psychological safety, reinforced by healthy team norms. **Psychological safety** is a term organizational researchers developed for teams in the workplace. Psychological safety is measured in four domains:

— attitude towards risk and failure

— open conversation

— willingness to help

— inclusivity

As a leader, you can only address team norms if the team feels psychologically safe. Let's cover what that means.

BUILD PSYCHOLOGICAL SAFETY

Researchers who study organizational development and team dynamics have spent decades identifying the norms that define a high functioning team. In an outcome rare for research in the social sciences, there is actually consensus and alignment across a variety of studies and research approaches.

The single most important factor that all healthy teams share is psychological safety. Researchers have broken down the idea into four key domains.

1. Attitude to Risk and Failure

The team sees failure as a necessary byproduct of growth and innovation, instead of something to be punished and avoided at all costs. The decade-long push to bring design thinking into many areas of organizational strategy has helped some teams learn to lean into experimentation with the expectation that some experiments will fail. It is the job of a good leader to help your team lean into discomfort and accept that sometimes they're going to drop the ball. Mature and psychologically safe teams embrace failure as a tool for growth, without blaming or leveraging failure against one another.

2. Open Conversation

Team members feel comfortable expressing concerns and reservations as they work together. They learn from one another and hear constructive feedback in the spirit it is intended.

One way leaders erode psychological safety is by refusing to take responsibility. You're going to take yourself with you, no matter where you go or what problem you tackle, so learn to welcome opportunities to grow your self-awareness: What do you gain when you're willing to be wrong?

3. Willingness to Help

The team has a spirit of being "in this together" and they easily pick up slack for the benefit of the whole. Team members do not take advantage of others.

When a team lacks this component, there is a general unwillingness to help others or to let others help, or taking responsibility for things that should belong to others. It's the job of the leader to incentivize genuine collaboration while setting boundaries and blocking power thieves.

4. Inclusivity

The team works hard to ensure all perspectives are represented, even from those who are not always first to speak.

Address these four areas of team dynamics, and you will go a long way to creating a work environment that is safe enough to begin changing team norms, the communication and collaboration processes that support psychological safety.

"Culture is how employees' hearts and stomachs feel about Monday morning on Sunday night."

—Bill Marklein

ADDRESS BROKEN TEAM NORMS

Once you begin to improve psychological safety, you can move to team norms, the day-in and day-out expectations and processes that allow people to work together toward shared goals.

Team norms and psychological safety go hand in hand. Teams with strong psychological safety have the skills to talk about and improve their team norms; unhealthy team norms can erode psychological safety and lead to lowered performance across the entire team.

Collaboration and communication are two common areas where team norms suffer. Let's explore why.

Fix broken collaboration processes. Remember, the research shows that people are willing to consider change when they feel part of a collaborative community bound by a compelling purpose.

One of the first steps in building a collaborative community is fixing broken processes for communication, collaboration and decision making, including meeting norms and calendar expectations.

Dr. Linda Hill refers to teams that have achieved this as "digitally mature organizations,"[23] and they can be judged on three basic characteristics:

1. A foundation of shared norms, including how they communicate and how they make decisions. Decisions are distributed rather than top-down and team members are invited to co-create change.

2. A "challenger mindset" and willingness to question/ disrupt, with a focus on continuous experimentation and learning.

3. Tools and time to support numbers one and two.

You and your team need a strong foundation of healthy collaboration norms to support your change initiative. Set up processes, workflows, and lines of decision-making authority to establish good communication. Often people confuse this setup work with the change initiative itself, but these steps actually support work delivery.

How This Works in the Real World

One team we worked with was attempting to take on a major change initiative without this foundation of healthy team norms.

The change involved rewriting and aligning success metrics and decision frameworks for approving major projects across departments. These departments were used to having autonomy. In theory, the proposed changes made rational sense. The existing process was inefficient and left each team on their own for raising capital.

The organization also had a culture of consensus, where everyone felt they had a right to be involved in every decision, leading to a ton of meetings and slow decision making.

The team had a clear proposed solution: align on what we're doing so we can be more effective. But the implementation had a few hurdles before the alignment could even start.

Teams had no time to work on this effort because their calendars were clogged with meetings. The tools used for communication and collaboration were specific to each department and there was no clear way to message across departments other than email. And team members expressed serious skepticism and resisted giving up their autonomy.

The first phase of their change initiative had to begin not with the change itself, but with rolling out a new communication platform and project management system so that the "real work" could begin. Unfortunately for their proposed timelines, working through these updates caused serious delays and distracted from the more significant change the leaders had been trying to achieve.

> Since collaborating on the new five-year vision couldn't begin until everyone got comfortable using Microsoft Teams and posting documents to SharePoint instead of sending by email the project took *much longer* than expected to get off the ground.

Ideally, the work to fix broken collaboration processes can happen both in advance of major change initiatives and also during the initiative. Part of shifting team norms is about *process* (policies, templates, etc.) but the success of a culture shift depends on the *people*. The change leader will need to take into account the organizational culture, individual mindsets and egos, and how the organization incentivizes team members to work together or look out for their own reputation.

With so many channels available to connect, one easy way to improve communication quickly is by defining the primary communication channels. Additionally, team members shouldn't waste time searching for shared documents and assets, so there must be an organized place where information is stored.

"There are four reasons to meet:
to decide, to learn,
to bond, and to do.
If it doesn't serve one of
those purposes, cancel it."

—Adam Grant

Fix broken communication processes. Emails, text, chat thread, meeting chats and side-of-the-desk chats all interrupting work can take hours each day. Teams need to know when and how each channel should be used to communicate most effectively. *(Download the Team Norms template at* changefatigue.com.*)*

Here are some areas where leaders need to work constantly to ensure the team is digitally mature.

— **Do team members use meetings effectively?** Are meetings focused on discussion, collaboration and decision making, or are they always dominated by a single presenter focused on sharing updates?

  • Are team members in control of their own calendars or are others allowed to fill their full workday?

  • Are they freely allowed to decline meetings where they feel they cannot add value?

— **Do team members know when and how to choose a communication channel?**

- Have leaders identified expectations for response time on emails, text messages, team chats, and other forms of communication?

- Are team members allowed to unplug and concentrate during the workday or are they expected to be immediately responsive?

— **Do team members know how to assign tasks to one another and check on the progress of collaborative efforts?**

- Is there a shared tool for accountability and visibility of collaborative work?

- Are all team members able to see the same view for transparency and reducing update meetings?

- Are team members accountable for deadlines and keeping their tasks updated in the system?

— **Can team members find the resources to do their work?** Is there a defined file structure that makes it obvious where this document belongs?

Think "spaghetti not confetti." Taking a broader view to think about your organization as a system will allow you to identify dependencies and requirements across different stakeholder groups. Ingrid Burkett from The

Australian Centre for Social Innovation uses a "spaghetti versus confetti" metaphor to help explain how teams need to think about change.[24] Confetti solutions are disconnected and often optimistically considered as a "magic bullet" that will just solve the whole problem. But organizations are often much more like a pile of spaghetti—complex, interconnected, and unlikely to be improved with one-off solutions.

Instead, think about consistently prioritizing strong collaborative relationships. Some teams approach their work with a more competitive than collaborative mindset. Information is not shared broadly, which often translates to duplication of effort, frustration, and inefficiencies. Isolated decisions lead to wasted time and effort.

As a change leader, take the system into account from the initial kickoff of the change so you can address the complexity across teams. This isn't just about happiness; it's about helping them understand how they drive value for the organization.

WHAT'S LOST: WHEN PSYCHOLOGICAL SAFETY AND HEALTHY TEAM NORMS ARE MISSING

Seventy-five percent of leaders overestimate the levels of psychological safety in their workplace. Just like self-awareness is a core skill for relationships generally, the leadership version is more like "team awareness." Are team members being honest with you about their experience of being on this team? Is it working for them? Are there areas of weakness the team could improve if they were brought into the open?

If you are realizing while reading this chapter that you're unsure whether psychological safety is an area of concern within your team, it's important to gather some data. Benchmark your team's psychological safety, either via a simple web survey or with the help of a team facilitator certified in helping with improvements (like the authors of this book).[25]

However you choose to move forward, don't overlook the negative impacts of neglecting these areas on team performance generally, and specifically on their ability to absorb and adopt change.

It becomes obvious when you consider two teams with opposite scores on these important benchmarks going through the same change.

Picture this... two communications teams at two different organizations. Team Alpha scores high on psychological safety and checks all the boxes for healthy team norms while Team Omega does not.

Both teams are tasked with implementing a new tool for storing and indexing all the knowledge assets of the organization, including sales materials, webinars, research reports, and more. Every department in the organization creates content that belongs in this new Knowledge Management tool. This effort will make things easier to find, reducing time wasted hunting for valuable information and eliminating duplicate work.

Management is very excited about these efficiencies, and the change leader within the communications department knows that their team will be one of the teams that benefits the most but will also have to do the most work.

Team Alpha approaches the challenge with a healthy attitude toward risk and failure. The head of Team Alpha welcomes their concerns as they brainstorm together on all the things that could go wrong in the project.

Everyone feels comfortable sharing their perspectives, even contrary views about whether this new tool is worth the effort. Members of Team Alpha volunteer to take on extra responsibilities to research alternatives and other team members step up to more daily responsibilities to make room for this additional set of tasks. They connect with experienced staff on their team and beyond who could have valuable input to refine the project plan, and they set up a communications and accountability plan and ensure they all agree on meeting schedules, communication strategies, and project management.

They also know that if one of the team members falls behind on their tasks or steps outside the team norms, they can gently remind and support them without making them feel criticized or excluded.

Team Omega is a different story. Team members have frequently been chastised or even punished for pushing back on assignments from "the top" and Team Omega's leader has made clear that this change is happening. Period.

Since it's clear that "failure is not an option," the team has only one choice: to follow instructions they know in their hearts just won't work. Extra tasks from this project pile up, but there is no open conversation about what can move to make room for this project.

Working longer hours on what feels like a doomed project brings resentment and disengagement. The team leader excludes valuable input from experienced team members because the plan has no room for adjustment.

The energy on the project is sluggish, and everyone does their tasks in their own way, independent from others, missing opportunities to learn from each other and to reduce duplication of effort. Documents are saved in siloes that others can't access, some team members are in email, some are in the organization chat, some are adding tasks to the project management tool, and everyone is frustrated with everyone else. The project feels like a huge burden with no reward, and slowly the output grinds to a halt.

No matter what the change is, it's easy to see that Team Alpha has a culture that is ready to adapt and evolve. Team Omega is going to struggle. The impact of psychological safety and healthy team norms on team performance simply cannot be overstated, and every leader at every level can work to benchmark and improve, even in the absence of a change initiative on the horizon.

That said, teams often lack the budget and focus to carve out time for these improvements until something big is at stake. In our work as change facilitators, we help teams identify their cultural challenges and work to improve them using a change initiative as the catalyst and the reason for improvement.

So, Team Omega might get a change facilitator who is supposed to be focused on implementation, but may also get pointers and coaching along the way on tools and processes to improve the culture and leave the team with not just a new knowledge management tool, but new knowledge about themselves and the way they work.

► MILESTONE ACHIEVED

Psychological Safety Benchmarked and Healthy Team Norms in Place

TAKEAWAYS FOR HEALTHY TEAMS

It's important to realize that just like with our physical bodies, getting healthier takes time. Rushing the process can backfire. Go slowly, and make sure to acknowledge even small victories along the way.

Encourage, don't praise. Praise is a (sometimes condescending) judgment, while encouragement compliments the effort and investment. Look for ways to authentically acknowledge good work across the team and reward in ways that are meaningful for the recipient.

Take time for celebration. You get more of what you measure and celebrate. Gratitude is a source of inspiration; shared expressions of gratitude are a base for celebration. Be sure to celebrate ancillary goals and success that are less noticeable such as fewer meetings this month or less time spent hunting for the right version of the file. These wins are sometimes harder to see and often are not official milestones in the change initiative, but celebrating them can give the team a boost to stay on track.

CONCLUSION

Now What?
Next Steps and Working with a
Change Facilitator

By now we hope you realize that leading effective change requires not just a clear definition of the problem and solution but also an intentional examination of who is going to be impacted and how those stakeholders will make or break your plans. Although leaders tend to manage change on an organizational level, it is through individual change that the broader change actually happens.

Persuade *and* convince. This concept from best-selling author Seth Godin sums up the difference between trying to convince someone that your point is *accurate* and persuading them to really *believe.*

"Persuasion appeals to the emotions and to fear and to the imagination. Convincing requires a spreadsheet or some other rational device. It's much easier to persuade someone if they're already convinced, if they already know the facts. But it's impossible to change someone's mind merely by convincing them of your point."[26]

Nothing lasting can happen if you as the change leader and the highly impacted stakeholders are not aligned. We've watched this alignment phase fail far too often. Leaders work with experts to craft an (often expensive) transformation strategy that seems like it will work on paper, but the team is not aligned and feels forced into change, so they resist. They don't feel heard when they try to speak up about risks to the initiative, get resources, or understand how they're supposed to fit this innovation into their workday. The transformation stalls, leaders pause to re-evaluate, priorities shift, and eventually the cycle is repeated with a new expert transformation strategy on the horizon.

It can even go wrong from the bottom up. A team member may have a great idea for doing things differently but only gets leaders to (half-heartedly) allow them to pilot a solution on their own time. This is a clear signal that the leaders don't agree on the problem or don't believe in the solution, and the pilot project is likely doomed from the start.

Change is hard work. If leaders and team members truly want to break the cycle of false solutions and put their energy into a change having a better chance of success, they need to stay in this uncomfortable space. When people are defensive or silent, change leaders need to be willing to start difficult conversations based on the underlying problem.

For many leaders, adoption—just getting them to start doing the new behavior—is the primary goal at launch. However, sustaining the new behavior ought to be the true measure of success. In other words, if everyone goes back to doing it "the old way" as soon as the launch is over, and the change has failed even if the launch was successful.

To support this long-term behavior change, identify what supporting behaviors need to evolve: mindset, team values, or work habits. Also, consider if there are training needs to support the new processes, workflows, and practices. Creating a feedback loop and communicating how the team is performing helps make these new ways of working stick.

Working with a change facilitator. So you read the paragraph above and you wholeheartedly agree but... you still aren't sure how to figure out what that means for your team, your timeline, and your change. As you've seen through the examples we've shared, change can be complicated. An experienced change facilitator specializes in defining:

— the project or program constraints, including defining the real problem you are trying to solve.

— the big-picture, systems thinking that will uncover key relationships to sponsor, and drive change.

— the connection and feedback required to mitigate resistance.

— the individual motivations and work balancing.

— the level of trust, communication and psychological safety the team brings to the start of the change, and how to support growth.

It doesn't have to be big and expensive to address these challenges. The more expensive choice is to push a change forward that has low odds of success. This costs money directly in implementation and training, and indirectly because of the costs of change fatigue and lost social capital.

With the help of a change facilitator, early intervention in small consistent ways can help nudge change efforts in the right direction.

When to get help. If you need help understanding change requirements, key decision making and problem-solving roles, and the importance of individual contributions, while managing the process, a change facilitator can help. Change facilitators also provide guidance for:

— teams struggling to work together.

— exposing and engaging with obstacles.

— identifying outcomes that will boost change adoption.

The independent perspective of a change facilitator also reduces bias by working to capture themes, actions, discussion points, and insights without filtering them through the lens of a stakeholder.

Jenny and Melissa specialize in getting change initiatives back on track and building stronger teams through team facilitation, collaboration, psychological safety benchmarking, and other organizational development and coaching strategies. Visit changefatigue.com for resources, webinars, workshops, and other ways to work with the authors.

ABOUT THE AUTHORS

Jenny Magic and Melissa Breker have been collaborating on consulting projects and sharing the speaking stage since 2015. With decades of experience guiding teams through digital transformation, they decided in 2020 to create an official collaboration and started building towards this book in your hand.

MEET JENNY MAGIC, CPC

Jenny Magic brings almost 20 years of marketing transformation experience to her change management and team performance practice, Better Way to Say It. One of her clients dubbed her a "marketing therapist" years ago for her ability to get a dysfunctional team back on track, and the label stuck.

She relies on her facilitation skills to build consensus around the tactical areas—processes, workflows and technology—that allow change to actually stick.

She has led extended projects with Sesame Workshop, AARP, Citrix, Prudential, Acxiom, Alcon, Purdue University, Experian, US Bank, Cisco and many others.

She is a certified professional coach as well as an external practitioner for the Fearless Organization, using the Psychological Safety Index as a team performance benchmark.

Connect with Jenny: Linkedin.com/in/JennyLMagic
Twitter.com/JennyLMagic

MEET MELISSA BREKER, ACC, BIBR, PROSCI

Melissa is a facilitator, coach, and change management consultant with over 20 years of experience applying strategic thinking to digital projects.

As a thinking partner, she inspires new ways of connecting and communicating to improve how teams and people work together. From difficult conversations to new ideas, Melissa drives practical transition and adoption of business and people change.

She works closely with teams to support leadership around change and helps organizations deliver customer and employee experiences during times of transition.

Melissa is a certified ICF coach and international speaker. She has facilitated workshops and led projects with Samsung, Teck Resources, TELUS, Experian, BC Hydro, and Wells Fargo Retirement Banking Group.

Connect with Melissa: Linkedin.com/in/MelissaBreker
Twitter.com/MelissaBreker

REFERENCE

Endnotes

1 "2022 Alixpartners Disruption Index." Insights & Impact, AlixPartners, 2022, https://docs.alixpartners.com/view/379117058/40/.

2 "4Q22 CFO Signals Full Report," Deloitte, 2022, https://www2.deloitte.com/content/dam/Deloitte/us/Documents/us-xa-4q22-cfo-signals-full-report.pdf.   .

3 Kotter, John P. 2012. Leading Change, With a New Preface by the Author. Harvard Business Press.

4 Hill, Linda A., Greg Brandeau, Emily Truelove, and Kent Lineback. 2014. Collective Genius: The Art and Practice of Leading Innovation. Harvard Business Press.

5 "2022 Alixpartners Disruption Index." Insights & Impact, AlixPartners, 2022, https://docs.alixpartners.com/view/379117058/40/.

6 Farnsworth, Bryn. "What Is Participant Bias? (And How to Defeat It)." Imotions. January 23, 2023. https://imotions.com/blog/learning/best-practice/participant-bias/.

7 Kriglstein, Robin. "Designing for Behavior Change." Invited Talk at Ethos at Thirteen23, February 4, 2020.

8 Adapted from IDEAU. Boyle, Brendan. "Brainstorming." IDEAU, 2019. https://www.ideou.com/pages/brainstorming.

9 Gray, Dave. "How-Now-Wow Matrix – Gamestorming," January 5, 2011. https://gamestorming.com/how-now-wow-matrix.

10 Lewin, Kurt (May 1943). "Defining the 'Field at a Given Time'". Psychological Review. 50(3): 292–310. Republished in Resolving Social Conflicts & Field Theory in Social Science. Washington, D.C.: American Psychological Association, 1997.

11 Gray, Dave, Sunni Brown, and James Macanufo. Gamestorming: A Playbook for Innovators, Rulebreakers, and Changemakers. O'Reilly Media, Inc., 2010

12 Prosci, "Best Practices in Change Management," October 11, 2022, https://www.prosci.com/resources/articles/change-management-best-practices.

13 Gregory M. Vecchia, Vincent B. Van Hasseltb, and Stephen J. Romanoc, "Crisis (hostage) negotiation: current strategies and issues in high-risk conflict resolution," Aggression and Violent Behavior 10 (2005)

14 Barker, Eric, and Chris Voss. "Hostage Negotiation Interview." Barking Up The Wrong Tree (blog), n.d. https://bakadesuyo.com/full-chris-interview/

15 Prosci, "Best Practices in Change Management," October 11, 2022, https://www.prosci.com/resources/articles/change-management-best-practices.

16 Armenakis, A.A., Harris, S.G., and Mossholder, K.W. 1993. "Creating Readiness for Organizational Change." Human Relations, 46: 681-703.

17 Prosci, "Best Practices in Change Management,"

18 Lerner, Jennifer S., Ye Li, Piercarlo Valdesolo, and Karim S. Kassam. "Emotion and Decision Making." Annual Review of Psychology 66, no. 1 (January 5, 2015): 799–823. https://doi.org/10.1146/annurev-psych-010213-115043.

19 Covey, Stephen M. R. "The Speed of Trust: The One Thing That Changes Everything," n.d. https://www.speedoftrust.com/.

20 Albert Mehrabian, Silent Messages: Implicit Communication of Emotions and Attitudes, 2nd ed, 1981.

21 David Rock, Four Acronyms to Help Understand Work and

Motivations: https://neuroleadership.com/your-brain-at-work/neuroscience-future-of-work-acronyms

22 Reilly, Tanya. "Being Glue." noidea.dog, May 10, 2019. https://noidea.dog/glue.

23 Linda Annette Hill et al., Collective Genius: The Art and Practice of Leading Innovation (Harvard Business Press, 2014).

24 Burkett, Ingrid and Australian Centre for Innovation. "Evaluating Systems Change." Australia, n.d. https://youtu.be/N2VI-YZCDIDU. 19 May 2017

25 PSI: Anonymous Team and Organization Scan," n.d. https://fearlessorganization.com/engage/psi-anonymous-team-and-organization-scan.

26 "Persuade vs. Convince," Seth's Blog, December 17, 2020, https://seths.blog/2012/11/persuade-vs-convince.